The Field Guide

THE FIELD GUIDE

First published as *The Beginner's Guide to Crop Circle Making*
by FE³ for the Fete Worse Than Death, 1994.
Second Edition published 2004 by Circlemakers Press, 2004.
Third Edition, *The Field Guide*, published 2006 by Strange Attractor Press, 2006.

ISBN: 0954805429

STRANGE ATTRACTOR PRESS
BM SAP
LONDON, WC1N 3XX

WWW.STRANGEATTRACTOR.CO.UK
WWW.CIRCLEMAKERS.ORG

THE FIELD GUIDE

THE ART, HISTORY AND PHILOSOPHY OF CROP CIRCLE MAKING

BY ROB IRVING
AND JOHN LUNDBERG

EDITED BY MARK PILKINGTON

WITH CONTRIBUTIONS FROM
ROD DICKINSON AND WIL RUSSELL

The Field Guide

To Doug, Dave and all circlemakers past, present and future.

ACKNOWLEDGMENTS

Rob Irving: I would like to thank Denis Robertson, Terry Wilson, Mark Barnes and Dave Savage for their helpful insights and way with words, some of which I stole. And also Leslie, for all my time I've stolen from her by sitting before this screen.

Mark Pilkington: Thanks to John, Rob, Rod and Wil – The Circlemakers – for drawing me into their world; and to Richard Bancroft, Alyssa Joye and Val Stevenson for their supernatural proof-reading abilities.

Cover Design by John Lundberg.

THE FIELD GUIDE

CONTENTS

The Field Guide

INTRODUCTION

There are probably fewer than 50 circlemakers currently active in the world. A number of them have been involved in the creation of this book.

In fact, we're very happy to be able to present the accumulated knowledge and experience of three generations of circlemakers, covering three decades of activity. John Lundberg's interview with original crop artist Doug Bower – the man who started it all – provides an insight into the origins of the form; our principal author, Rob Irving, was a bête noire on the scene during its heyday at the start of the 1990s, making apparent truths that others were still determined to avoid; while the Circlemakers themselves have continued to push the envelope of what is possible in the field since the middle of that same decade.

This is actually the third edition of this book, which began as a shortened version of the "Roll Your Own" section in 1994. A limited run of 100 copies was produced in 2004 as *The Beginners' Guide To Crop Circle Making*, and now we present this new, considerably expanded publication.

While several forests worth of books have been written about what the crop circles might mean, the necessary level of secrecy surrounding the true force behind the formations means that this is the first book written entirely from the circlemakers' perspective. Simultaneously a history, a how-to guide and an exploration of why people make crop circles and how others respond to them, we hope that our book will inspire new generations of crop artists to fashion stompers of their own and amaze us with their creations.

As circlemakers, we feel confident that crop formations will continue to appear in England's fields, and those of other nations, until the end of time. However, should they ever stop showing up, then perhaps some day in the not-too-distant future someone will find this book, rediscover a lost artform and wonder will once more pour forth from the fields.

Mark Pilkington
Strange Attractor Press
London, England 2006

The Field Guide

INTRODUCTION TO THE 2004 EDITION

"I don't want to get into a philosophical discussion with you, but they can't all be hoaxes" – policeman to Rob Irving, 1992. Quoted in *Round in Circles* by Jim Schnabel.

I first experienced the transformative power of crop circles about five years ago. Myself, a friend, Rob Irving – author of the tome you are wise enough to be reading now – and another circlemaker were sitting quietly in the corner of Alton Barnes' East Field, a site traditionally reserved for each year's show-stopping formation. 1998 was no exception. A huge radial pattern, quite possibly the work of one of our party, engulfed much of the field. Around its perimeter that fine summer afternoon stood about two hundred people, arms outstretched, eyes turned upwards to the sky, preparing to receive the blessing of a Native American shaman of questionable provenance.

As we sat taking in the peaceful spectacle, a malevolent hissing began to emanate from our side of the Circle of Love. What sounded like an angry mongoose was, in fact, a well known croppy (anyone involved in the circles business can be referred to as a croppy), a prominent local land-owner and an active proponent of the circles mystery. This woman, who shall remain nameless, turned repeatedly to hiss in our direction, a geyser of hate in an oasis of love.

Somewhere in this book, Rob Irving calls crop circles "the most powerful art form of the 20th century" and what you are holding is a book of power, its signs and symbols as potent as those of any mediæval grimoire. As well as how to make your own crop formations, you will also learn about psychology and semantics (when is a formation "genuine"?); belief and deception; fraud and physiology; the power of language; the workings of the media; and that some people will believe anything if you tell them it in the right way, even if it runs contrary to all the available evidence. In flights of fantasy I like to imagine that one year the various circle making teams will agree not to produce any formations, presenting those who feed off their work with an interesting dilemma: provide a suitable explanation for the dearth of formations - or make your own.

The formations themselves are an art form, involving meticulous planning and back-breaking labour, and it is high time that they were duly recognised as such. The crop circle phenomenon is another component of this art, and is all about people – the people who make the circles, the people who study them, and the people who respond to them. It's a tightly intertwined network of symbiotic relationships, in which information and influence flow in all directions. Without the circlemakers there would be no circles for the "cerealogists" to study, yet without "cerealogists" to publicise the circles then it is unlikely that we'd continue to see so many spectacular designs appearing in the fields each year.

Of course, mysteries do remain. If the reports of spontaneous healings, woundings, equipment failures and the like are to be taken at face value – and, experience suggests that they should be examined extremely carefully before doing so – then the power of

The Field Guide

the circles continues to be worthy of serious study. If, again, these reports are true, then such incidents should be considered alongside similar phenomena reported at other of the world's holy sites.

The human organism has yet to give up all its secrets but, with this book, the Circlemakers have. Use the information it contains wisely and responsibly. If you are preparing to make the transition from observer to participant in this enduringly fascinating phenomenon, consider carefully the consequences of your actions. There are powerful forces at work out there and many lives have been changed – not always for the better – through dealing with them. You have been warned.

See you in the field.

Mark Pilkington
London, England 2003.

PROLOGUE

"One measures a circle, beginning anywhere" Charles Fort

Prologue

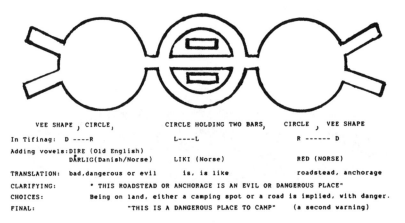

	VEE SHAPE , CIRCLE,	CIRCLE HOLDING TWO BARS,	CIRCLE , VEE SHAPE
In Tifinag:	D ----R	L----L	R ------ D
Adding vowels:	DIRE (Old English)		
	DÅRLIG(Danish/Norse)	LIKI (Norse)	RED (NORSE)
TRANSLATION:	bad,dangerous or evil	is, is like	roadstead, anchorage
CLARIFYING:		* THIS ROADSTEAD OR ANCHORAGE IS AN EVIL OR DANGEROUS PLACE"	
CHOICES:		Being on land, either a camping spot or a road is implied, with danger.	
FINAL:		"THIS IS A DANGEROUS PLACE TO CAMP" (a second warning)	

2

Summer of 1991 ended in ultimate frustration for Erik Beckjord, the charismatic American crop circles researcher, alien linguist, Loch Ness Monster hunter and founder of San Francisco's Crypto-Phenomena and World's Biggest Ball O'String Museum. Having successfully deciphered the codes of the crop circlemakers, writ large across the Wiltshire landscape in giant "pictogram" arrangements of circles, rings and lines, when he tried to talk to them in English, they answered him in Latin.

Beckjord was used to seeing form where others could not, and he saw in the Wiltshire pictograms a curious blend of Korean characters and an ancient African Berber alphabet called Tifinag, which had been adopted and adapted long ago, claimed Beckjord,

THE FIELD GUIDE

by Nordic travellers. Accordingly, each single geometric element represented the English equivalent of a consonant, with the vowels remaining silent and unseen. Once he had identified the correct consonants, by selectively inserting the corresponding vowels Beckjord found that he could construct whole words and sentences. For example, using this method he translated a sequence of circles and rings found near Winchester, as

TH(I)S (I)S (A) D(A)NG(E)R(OU)S PL(A)C(E) T(O) C(A)MP

Other messages echoed a distant mythic past:

TH(I)S (I)S TH(E) PL(A)C(E) (O)F TH(E) D(E)V(I)L

TH(E) TR(IA)L BY TH(E) L(A)W S(A)Y TH(E) S(E)CR(E)T WR(I)T(I)NGS

TH(E) DR(A)G(O)N FR(O)M P(E)G(A)S(U)S, FR(O)M TH(E) (OU)TS(I)D(E), C(O)M(E)S T(O) G(I)V(E) (A) TR(IA)L T(O) TH(E) (EA)RTH-GL(O)B(E)

(The interpretation of "Earth-globe" must have come after Beckjord's lecture to a crowd in an upstairs room in a pub in Glastonbury, Somerset, that year, because during this talk he translated the letters RTH as representing TH(O)R. It was only after someone in the audience suggested the more eco-friendly derivative (EA)RTH, that Beckjord accepted an alternative.)

By the time of the impending harvest, it was obvious that Beckjord was being hindered by an old fashioned British reserve in accepting his translations at face value. Like most scientists, Beckjord strove for certainty, and usually arrived at it before anyone else, but unlike others he accepted nothing less. And besides, for someone as self-assured as him – he was known as "Erik the Viking" to his admirers – the alien messages were often far too prosaic for him to comprehend. Why would the circlemakers go to all the trouble of writing something so ambiguous and mundane? Who were the messages aimed at, if not him?

Impatient with these limitations, and wanting *something important that*

Eric Beckjord *prepares his message.*

everyone can understand to show at his museum in California, Beckjord decided to take the initiative and send a message to the circlemakers directly, in plain English. Having paid off a farmer for the use of a field and hired an industrial strimmer, Beckjord and two volunteers spent a warm afternoon cutting and clearing wheat. Finally, letters took

form, and then words. Like the enigmatic Nasca lines in the Peruvian desert, and as with the crop pictograms that Beckjord was hoping to emulate, the message was properly visible only from above. It read, simply, "TALK TO US".

An answer came a week later. It was etched into a wheat field below Milk Hill, just a few miles from the site of Beckjord's plea. Unfortunately, far from the hoped-for dialogue in English, the message was not in any language that even Beckjord understood, nor anyone else. At least, initially.

"Talk *to us."*

5

Prologue

OI ICNUCIII NLNƆƆNI IO

The Milk Hill Script *(above)*, as it became known, ran parallel to the "tram" or tractor lines used by the farmer to spray without damaging the crop. It consisted of 17 characters – some, vertical lines, others connected by horizontal lines to make box-like shapes. At each end of the script was a ring. Whatever the message was trying to tell researchers, all agreed that its placement on the tramlines, as if doubly underlined, made a definitive translation all the more urgent.

With Beckjord at a loss, and now lost to California, the first to interpret the script was Michael Green, the bumptious Chairman of the newly-formed Centre for Crop Circles Studies. According to Green, the scripture had been delivered in an archaic form of Hebrew, favoured by Atlanteans. Reading from right to left with the tramlines underneath, Green's translation read "PHEHTHI" or "PTAH", then "EA-CHECHE" or "EA-ENKI". As PTAH meant "ancient god of creation" and "EA-ENKI" translated as "ancient god of wisdom" or "friend of the people", the true meaning of the message, asserted Green, triumphantly, was "THE CREATOR, WISE AND LOVING". It was scripture from the one true God, which only he was able to understand. Unfortunately for Green, his eminence crumbled when others of a more mediate, earthly eminence had different ideas.

THE FIELD GUIDE

Professor Gerald Hawkins, author of *Stonehenge Decoded* and other works on ancient science, had already noted in simple configurations of circles an inbuilt Euclidean geometry. He even applied his own unique theorems, showing a relationship between the circles and the diatonic scale. It was assumed from this that the circlemakers must have had advanced knowledge of these unique theorums in order to make the circles, and, therefore, this excluded humans.

Professor Hawkins now turned his analytical attentions to the Milk Hill script, supported by a team of 12 scholars. Their first translation was less than promising; it read "AH WELL". While some may have accepted a certain truth to this, Hawkins and his team pressed on, eventually announcing success. To start with, said the report, the script was framed within a set of assumed parameters:

1 - The circlemakers mark the message with breaks.

2 - The twin lines mark the word breaks.

3 - It is an exact character-by-character substitution code.

4 - The tramline marks the bottom of the characters.

5 - The message comprises two words, or two numbers.

6 - There are no abbreviations.

7 - The message is cognisable.

As no two cognisable numbers could be found from the cipher, they turned to words…

Prologue

after searching 18,000 common phrases in 42 languages, the first word, with its double letter and beginning and ending with the same letter, is 'OPPONO'. This is Latin for 'I oppose'. To be cognisable, the verb needs an object - the accusative case. The second word ends in O-blank, which can be only 'OS', the accusative plural. The only word possible seems to be 'ASTOS', plural of 'astus', meaning 'acts of craft and cunning'. The Milk Hill writing then translates as 'I oppose acts of craft and cunning'.

"We may tentatively add 'knowledge of Latin' to the so-called intellectual profile of the Circlemaker", concluded Hawkins.

We naturally tend to view the world, and even foreign worlds, within our own frame of reference. But we have also come to expect a higher degree of lateral thinking from those who have enjoyed lengthier educations, assuming scholars to have learned to see more, not less. Like priests, we place them beyond human fallibility. But even the most educated amongst us demonstrate a peculiar blindness to simple solutions. Perhaps even more so; it may be that the halls of academia serve as a protective firewall against the infinite jests of the outside world.

The same applies, of course, to would-be intellectuals. No commentary or history of the crop circles phenomenon would be complete without reference to the type of individual that unnecessarily overcomplicates solutions to simple problems in order to avoid challenging their existing beliefs. This is all the easier when such individuals form themselves into groups. But more on that later. Meanwhile, it is common for those who have not learned to avoid the pitfalls of paranormal research to assume that a little intellectualism is a good thing. This can lead to vast castles of the mind being built on the sandiest of foundations. If Hawkins represented the former, blinded to the obvious by his own intellect, Dutch crop circles researcher Robert Boerman's Milk Hill excursion was a fine example of the latter.

With Green's Hebrew/Atlantean translation established in his mind, Boerman held the script to a mirror, revealing a further message: "A new breed of people". "I began to understand the complexity of the Milk Hill scripture", wrote Boerman. Not only did the second revelation confirm the first, but it revealed a deeper truth. "All I could say was this is exactly right," he continues, "because 'Phehthi or Ptah, Ea-cheche or Ea-Enki' (in ancient times also known as Ea, Enki or Ptah) was the ancient god who, according to old Sumerian cuneiform clay tablets, was responsible for the creation of Homo Sapiens." To cut a long story short, the biblical Adam was "a worker" devised by Enki, an Anunnaki scientist of the pre-human era.

Where Charles Fort teased that earthlings were merely the property of higher beings, Green's analysis seemed to bear it out, and Boerman's confirmed it. The circle-

Prologue

makers were an advanced, supreme race – Gods! – announcing their return.

Confronted with all these academic interpretations we thought we would try our own. Viewing the script as sitting *below* the tramlines, then reading the characters as if they represent the lower half of a message, written according to the historical context and location in which the script was found, ie 20th Century English, but split widthwise – where, for example, E is represented by an angular C, D is U, S is a back-to-front C and L is of course L – and, as with Hawkins' criteria, if we assume the rings at each end mark the beginning and closing of the message, then add a "key", this being the dormant top half of the script, the message reads:

●MEAOENTALHSSHIT●

Dr Terence Meaden was a one-time professor of physics who went on to specialise as a meteorologist, running a small office in Bradford-on-Avon, Wiltshire, advising companies about the effects of tornadoes. He also edited and published the respected *Journal of Meteorology* from the same office.

One day in August, 1980, Meaden was contacted by a group of local ufologists who were investigating a crop circle found on a farm near the Wiltshire town of Westbury, eight miles away. It was the latest of three similar circles in the same area, the others by

Dr Terence *Meaden in 1992.*

now harvested. Considering all the possibilities of how the circles got there – extraterrestrial spacecraft, young farmers, helicopter downdraft – the team decided to contact Dr Meaden and ask if the cause could somehow be weather-related. Sure enough, after visiting the circle, Meaden hypothesised that its proximity to the steep slope of nearby White Horse Hill could have affected the surrounding airflow, causing an eddy or whirlwind to stabilise for long enough to leave a circular mark in the crop. This would also explain how each of the three circles had manifested in around the same place. Meaden outlined the theory in a

Prologue

subsequent issue of the *Journal of Meteorology.*

As time went by and single circles formed into patterns, and the number and complexity of the patterns increased, Meaden adapted his theory accordingly. By 1991, the rare eddy that could plausibly flatten a single circle had now mutated into a luminous electro-magneto-hydrodynamic, battery draining, temporal-lobe-epilepsy-inducing force field with a penchant for symbolism. He called it a "plasma vortex".

On the night of 11th July that same year, Rita Goold was out watching the fields near Alton Barnes, Wiltshire, the hub of crop circles activity, when she became the first and only person to witness a plasma vortex in all its glory. Dr Meaden rushed to publish her account in the *Journal of Meteorology:*

> *Suddenly, at 2.55 a.m., birds began singing which heightened our alertness and made us check wrist watches. It was soon quiet again, but at 3.00 a.m., almost exactly, I spotted a tube of light to the northeast descending vertically beneath a cloud in that part of the sky. Most of the remainder of the sky was clear and starry. The tube extended steadily in length as we watched, and its milky-white colour seemed to be due to a self-luminoscity like one might expect from the electrical effect known as plasma. As it came down against the black sky and neared the ground, the tube began to broaden, and branched out to give two opposed arms, as indicated in the drawing, forming a design in the*

air with rounded ends. Then the tube dissipated from the top downwards, and disappeared into the horizontal arms which themselves proceeded towards the ground out of sight beyond the hill peaks. No noise was heard. The whole phenomenon lasted about six seconds."

The trio of observers used their fingers held at arm's length to estimate angular dimensions of the phenomenon. Using these figures and the known distances of the surrounding hills, G.T. Meaden estimated the distance of the phenomenon at 1,400 meters; the width of the tube at 16 meters; and the width of the entire luminous mass at roughly 100 meters.

(Goold, Rita L.; *Observation of a Luminous-Tube Phenomenon at Alton Barnes, 12 July 1991,* Journal of Meteorology, UK, 16:274, 1991.)

During the 1980s, ex-theatre artistic director Rita Goold *(left)* had acquired a reputation within the Spiritualist community as the most powerful physical materialisation medium in the UK. Her seances were held in darkness, and

Prologue

she would manifest numerous characters from the afterlife, having them put on luminous costumes so that sitters could see them, proving their materiality. One, Raymond, the son of noted scientist Sir Oliver Lodge, had been killed in action during the First World War at the tender age of 17, but now regularly gallivanted around Rita's living room in full dress uniform and luminous trimmings. Another regular guest was Helen Duncan, the last person to be prosecuted under the Witchcraft Act in 1946. According to Rita, the coroner's report might not have said as much, but she knew from Helen herself exactly how she had died: internal injuries caused by "ectoplasmic splashback" during a police raid.

Rita attracted the interest of Professor Archie Roy, a physicist from Glasgow University. Roy wanted to scientifically prove the afterlife by the use of infra-red cameras during her seances; alas, however, at this point she suddenly retired from the scene. Later, following a chance meeting with leading crop circles experts in 1988, she re-emerged at a 10-day, 24-hour surveillance of a crop circle site in Hampshire: Operation White Crow.

On 17 June 1989, the final Saturday of a hitherto unsuccessful watch, crop circles expert and watch-leader Colin Andrews received an anomymous letter. It was written in a curious doggerel, informing him that if he really wanted to catch whatever was making the crop circles he would have to follow its instructions.

In your hands you have the key
To talk to us, we are so free

THE FIELD GUIDE

One soul is there…

A soul with the mind to link with the circlemakers. With Rita Goold's background as a famous psychic, reasoned Andrews, this had to mean her!

Get this Mind and Sit around
In quiet of dark upon the ground
Listen hard for every Sound
Not white of bird? But us Around.

Rita Goold *and friend on patrol.*

Just after midnight, Rita led Andrews and a few trusted pioneers to a field behind the surveillance site, where they found a fresh crop circle. The group sat together on the flattened barley, and in due course, as they settled into silence, Rita slipped into a trance. She whispered gently to the circlemakers to make themselves known, slowly repeating the request like a mantra.

A noise emerged from outside the circle. At first it sounded natural, like a chirruping cricket, but instead of the interrupted bursts of an orthopteran mating call it was more or less continuous. Now it was more of a reeling sound, which intensified until it seemed to envelop the group, surrounding them, invading their meditations…

Prologue

"But us Around"… The group was now entranced, and minutes seemed like hours, until eventually Rita spoke out, her voice penetrating the noise, asking whatever it was making it, if it understood her, to stop. And it *stopped!*

At that moment, if anyone there doubted that contact would be made with the circlemakers that night, this was proof enough, and nothing would persuade them otherwise.

But Colin Andrews had learned from experience that some of the associated phenomena that he had come across while investigating crop circles were so extraordinary that it was crucial to obtain tangible evidence where he could – otherwise who would believe him? As a respected speaker on the crop circle lecture circuit, how could he stand up and properly share these experiences?

So, a few hours after their encounter, armed with a dictaphone, Andrews returned to the site and captured the remnants of the noise, now fading into the distance. The tape can still be heard at crop circles conferences worldwide, portrayed as "the sound of the Circlemaker", but slowed down to a snail's pace for dramatic effect with every element of the trill now a lone, echoing entity… *plock… plock… plock.* Listeners are assured that no less an official body than NASA's Jet Propulsion Laboratory has analysed the sound and shown it to bear little, if any, similarity to the unique call of the Grasshopper Warbler, a bird known to inhabit southern English hedgerows during the summer months.

THE FIELD GUIDE

Grasshopper warbler

painting by Doug Bower.

The high, insect-like reeling song of the grasshopper warbler is the best clue to its presence. Even when you hear one it can be difficult to locate it due to the ventriloquial effect of its singing - a cricket-like trill lasting minutes. Best listened for between April and July, mostly at dawn and dusk but often through the night. If seen on migration it moves like a little mouse, creeping through the foliage." Royal Society for the Protection of Birds.

Prologue

In his earlier life, sexagenarian Doug Bower spent any spare time he had from running his art gallery and framing studio as a "twitcher" or bird watcher. But more than simply watching birds he liked to record them – his recordings can be found in various sound archives. He knew a *Locustella naevia* when he heard one. Even with his twitching heyday in the past, Doug still kept his equipment in the car, just in case...

Just in case, that was, the police happened to ask him what he was doing creeping around the countryside in the dead of night. On at least one occasion during the last 13 years this had made for a handy excuse, for twitching had now been eclipsed by Doug's covert life as a circlemaker.

Doug's generous, easygoing manner disguises a self-disciplined formality. His circlemaking activities were restricted to Friday evenings, week-in week-out, when he would meet his pal Dave Chorley and set off for the fields around Hampshire. But not this year. The pair had not spoken since Dave failed to turn up for drinks on Christmas Day the previous year.

On Saturday evenings, Doug and his wife Ilene liked to eat out, usually at a restaurant near their home in Southampton. On this occasion, however, Doug had contrived to drive 15 miles out of town to the Percy Hobbs, the closest pub to Cheesefoot Head, his favourite nocturnal stomping ground.

THE FIELD GUIDE

As they left the pub Ilene could see that something was troubling her husband, and she knew him well enough by now to know what it was. It was bad enough not having his pal around – since falling out with Dave, the number of circles in Hampshire had dropped considerably compared to previous years – but to miss the opportunity to make a special circle for Colin Andrews' watch… well, Doug found the idea especially depressing.

Rolling her eyes in mock impatience, and not for the first time, Ilene agreed to wait in the car as Doug parked it in the car park near the White Crow caravan, crept into the field behind it and swept a pristine circle into the barley…

Doug Bower *with field recording equipment.*

A PREHISTORY OF CROP CIRCLES

THE FIELD GUIDE

It is generally assumed that the crop circles are a recent phenomenon, one that emerged simultaneously with the first press reports in the early 1980s. A comparison of a post-war aerial survey of the British Isles with a contemporary online satellite map certainly supports this, and not one unambiguous photograph of a pre-1960s crop circle has come to light. But there's enough historical and anecdotal evidence of older formations to at least raise some interesting questions.

The known phenomenon begins, barely discernibly, in the murk of antiquity, at least a thousand years ago, with references to crop circles emerging through classical folklore. The total dependence of agrarian societies on successful harvests was reflected in their intimate relationship with their gods, communed through ritual and framed within myth. Many of these ancient magical practices have survived. In Britain, for example, a tradition continues of collecting the last sheaf from the summer's harvest to make corn dollies; these are believed to carry the cycle of growth through winter into spring. Perhaps the most familiar of these ancient deities is the Roman earth goddess Ceres, who gave birth to the term "cereal". Her daughter, Persephone, embodied the corn itself, and since she was snatched downwards by the King of the Underworld, any hole in a crop field is said to mark the spot where this happened. Even this early in our history of crop circles they were thought, at least conceptually, to represent portals to other worlds.

The concept of nature sprites inhabiting and working magic on our crops is also widespread across cultures. The figure of Robin Goodfellow, or Puck, is well-known in

Prehistory

England, immortalised by William Shakespeare in *A Midsummer Night's Dream*. But his Welsh counterpart *Pwca* and the Irish *Phuka* point to earlier origins (as do *puki* in Old Norse, *puke* in Swedish and *puge* in Danish), all deriving from "devil" or "evil spirit". It is thought that another is the English West Country native *pixie*. Tales of unwary travellers lured, or "pixie-led", through their darkest imaginings are an ideal metaphor for the pursuit of crop circles and its underlying tension between righteousness and mischief.

> *If any wanderers I meet*
> *that from their night-sports doe trudge home,*
> *With counterfeiting voyce I greet*
> *and cause them on with me to roame,*
> *Through woods, through lakes,*
> *Through bogs, through brakes, --*
> *Ore bush and brier with them I goe;*
> *I call upon Them to come on,*
> *And wend me, laughing ho, ho, ho!...*

> *By wels and gils in medowes greene,*
> *we nightly dance our heydegies*
> *And to our fairy King and Queene*
> *wee chant our moone-light harmonies.*

From a song about Robin Goodfellow (to the tune of **Dulcina**), *attributed to Ben Johnson, circa 1628.*

Bishop Agobard *and the cloudship occupants.*

There is an intriguing correlation between these kinds of accounts and stories featuring winds and whirlwinds. One of history's most vocal opponents of what he called "the tyranny of foolishness" was a clergyman named Agobard, Bishop of Lyon, who lived in the 9th century AD. He wrote no fewer than 22 books, including several treatises dispelling supernatural beliefs that he regarded as heretical (as opposed to the more divine supernatural beliefs that presumably he supported.) These included the popular notion that magicians and other evil-minded entities can manipulate and control inclement weather.

Prehistory

Writing *Against the foolish opinion of the masses about hail and thunder* (815 AD), Agobard reports how people believed that these "Tempestarii" had conjured cloud ships from Magonia, a far-off place in the skies. These manifested as fierce storms, and a ransom was demanded on behalf of the Magonians in the form of crops they had flattened. Bishop Agobard then tells of how he saved four prisoners from being put to death by an angry mob who had captured them, believing them to be Magonians. The Bishop does not specifically say that the gang was caught making a crop circle, though he does mention that the mob feared they were going to use magic to spoil the next year's harvest. "Things are believed by Christians of such absurdity as no one ever could aforetime induce the heathen to believe", observed the Bishop. In the eyes of the ecclesiastic authorities, however, the ramifications of this went too far, and Agobard would be persecuted by the very Establishment he stood for. He died in misery in 840.

Centuries later, the Church adopted the same ideas that Agobard had railed against. The principal text that codified beliefs about witchcraft and its powers was the *Malleus Maleficarum,* published in 1484. In the opening Papal Bull, Pope Innocent VIII recognises the power of witches in the destruction of crops, writing:

> *It has indeed lately come to Our ears ... many persons of both sexes ... have blasted the produce of the earth, the grapes of the vine, the fruits of the trees ... vineyards, orchards, meadows, pasture-land, corn, wheat, and all other cereals...*

The *Malleus* also contains a chapter describing in detail the witches' power over the weather, entitled "How they Raise and Stir up Hailstorms and Tempests, and Cause Lightning to Blast both Men and Beasts." By the 16th and 17th centuries it was widely accepted that tempestuous storms were the everyday *modus operandi* of the devilish.

It is cruelly ironic that after his death Bishop Agobard became a primary source of this mythology. A story attributed to Jacob Grimm (one of the Grimm brothers) telling of a storm of dislocated, discontent souls racing across the countryside in the form of a violent whirlwind, wreaking "havoc of a husbandman's crops", is believed to be lifted from Agobard's writings. Likewise, in a literary form of Chinese whispers spanning centuries, Agobard's reporting of popular belief in Magonia was subsequently adapted by the Abbot Mautfaucon de Villiers (1635-1665), whose version formed the basis of a 1964 article by W Raymond Drake, titled *Spacemen of the Middle Ages*. This version was then popularised by the respected UFO writer Jacques Vallée in his *Anatomy of a Phenomenon: Unidentified Objects in Space – a Scientific Appraisal*, and was then fed back into UFO/crop circle mythology as supporting evidence for the existence of "cloud ships" and their meteorological relationship to crop circles. One suspects that by this time the good Bishop was turning circles in his grave!

The earliest, most detailed evidence of a pre-20th century crop circle was discovered in the late 1980s, when a four-page 17th century pamphlet came to light in a book on Hertfordshire folklore. Dated 22nd August, 1678, its title-page was illustrated by a

26

woodcut showing a demonic figure cutting oats with a scythe. The cut stalks behind him appear to be laid out anticlockwise, forming a ringed circle or oval.

THE MOWING-DEVIL or, STRANGE
News Out of HARTFORD-SHIRE

Being a True Relation of a Farmer, who bargaining with a Poor Mower, about the Cutting down Three Half Acres of Oats: upon the Mower's asking too much the Farmer swore That the Devil should Mow it rather than He. And so it fell out, that very Night, the Crop of Oat shew'd as if it had been all of a Flame: but next morning appear'd so neatly mow'd by the Devil or some Infernal Spirit, that no Mortal Man was able to do the like.

27

Also, How the said Oats ly now in the Field, and the Owner has not Power to fetch them away.

Licensed, August 22, 1678 Men may dally with Heaven, and criticise on Hell, as Wittily as they please, but that there are really such places, the wise Dispensations of Almighty Providence does not cease continually to evince. For if by those accumulated circumstances which generally Induce us to the belief of anything beyond our senses, we may reasonably gather that there are certainly such things as DEVILS, we must necessarily conclude that these Devils have a Hell: and as

Prehistory

there is a Hell, there must be a Heaven, and consequently a GOD: and so all the Duties of Christian Religion as indispensable subsegments necessarily follow.

The first of which Propositions, this ensuing Narrative does not a little help to Confirm.

For no longer ago, than within the compass of the present Month of August, there hapned so unusual an Accident in Hartfordshire as is not only the general Discourse, and admiration of the whole County: but may for its Rarity challenge any other event, which has for these many years been product In any other County whatsoever. The story thus.

In the said County lives a Rich industrious Farmer, who perceiving a small Crop of his (of about three Half-Acres of Land which he had sowed with Oats) to be Ripe and fit for Gathering, sent to a poor Neighbour whom he knew worked commonly in the Summer-time at Harvest Labour to agree with him about Mowlng or Cutting the said Oats down. The poor man as it behoov'd Him endeavour'd to sell the Sweat of his Brows and Marrow of his Bones at as dear a Rate as reasonably he might, and therefore askt a good round Price for his Labour, which the Farmer taking some exception at, bid him much more under the usual Rate than the poor Man ask: for it: So that some sharp Words had past, when the Farmer told him he would Discourse with him no more about it.

THE FIELD GUIDE

Whereupon the honest Mower recollecting with himself, that if he undertook not that little Spot of Work, he might thereby lose much more business which the Farmer had to employ him in beside, ran after him, and told him, that, rather than displease him, he would do it at what rate In Reason he pleased: and as an Instance of his willingness to serve him, proposed to him a lower price, than he had Mowed for any time this Year before. The irritated Farmer with a stern look, and hasty gesture, told the poor man That the Devil himself should Mow his Oats before he should have anything to do with them, and upon this went his way, and left the sorrowful Yeoman, not a little troubled that he had disoblig'd one in whose Power it lay to do him many kindnesses.

But, however, in the happy series of an Interrupted prosperity, we may strut and plume our selves over the miserable Indingencies of our necessitated Neighbours, yet there is a just God above, who weighs us not by our Bags, nor measures us by our Coffers: but looks upon all men Indifferently as the common sons of Adam: so that he who carefully Officiates that rank or Station wherein the Almighty has plac't him, tho' but a mean one, is truly more worthy the Estimation of all men, then he who is prefer'd to superior dignities, and abuses them: And what greater abuse than the contempt of Men below him: the relief of whose common necessities is none of the least Conditions whereby he holds all his Good things: which when that Tenure is forfeited by his default. He may justly expect some Judgement to ensue: or else that those riches whereby he prides himself so extravagantly may

Prehistory

shortly be taken from him.

We will not attempt to fathom the cause, or reason of, Preternatural events: but certain we are, as the most Credible and General Relation can Inform us, that same night this poor Mower and Farmer parted, his Field of Oats was publickly beheld by several Passengers to be all of a Flame, and so continued for some space, to the great consternation of those that beheld it.

Which strange news being by several carried to the Farmer next morning, could not but give him a great curiosity to go and see what was become of his Crop of Oats, which he could not imagine, but what was totally devour'd by those ravenous Flames which were observed to be so long resident on his Acre and a half of Ground.

Certainly a reflection on his sudden and Indiscreet expression (That the Devil should Mowe his Oats before the poor Man should have anything to do with them) could not but on this occasion come into his Memory. For if we will but allow our selves so much leisure, to consider how many hits of providence go to the production of one Crop of Corn, such as the aptitude of the Soyl, the Seasonableness of Showers, Nourishing Solstices and Salubrious Winds, etc., we should rather welcome Maturity with Devout Acknowledgements than prevent our gathering of it by profuse washes.

THE FIELD GUIDE

But not to keep the curious Reader any longer in suspense, the Inquisitive Farmer no sooner arriv'd at the place where his Oats grew, but to his admiration he found the Crop was cut down ready to his hands; and [as] if the Devil had a mind to shew his dexterity in the art of Husbandry, and scorn'd to mow them after the usual manner, he cut them in round circles, and plac't every straw with that exactness that it would have taken up above an Age for any Man to perform what he did that one night: And the man that owns them is as yet afraid to remove them.

FINIS

The temptation to accept this account as an historical record is understandable – indeed, many crop circles researchers have done so, one even describing it as a "news report" – because it would support the position that crop circles have appeared continuously for centuries. Furthermore, some details of the story are consistent with modern-day observations; could "all of a Flame" allude to a luminous whirlwind or the balls of light witnessed in and around modern crop circles? Certainly, the story contains convincing authenticating details, and some historians may rightfully argue that without trusting such material it would be difficult to have *any* knowledge of history.

But in a broader cultural and political context, the tale is consistent with a particular form of propaganda that was disseminated during the time of the Civil War, the following

Prehistory

interregnum and into the period of Restoration. It was an era of acute religious intolerance and superstition, in which a climate of fear led to the persecution of thousands of people for witchcraft and sorcery. Many were put to death, most were acquitted, but the beliefs that fuelled the hysteria continued long into the 18th century.

A recent study by a Harvard academic casts the Mowing Devil story in a different light. Emily Oster has shown significant correlations between witch-hunts and trials and the economic downturns brought on by decreases in temperature, resulting in crop failures and food shortages. The most active period of the witchcraft trials coincides with a period of lower than average temperature known to climatologists as the "Little Ice Age" (1645-1715). Why this occurred is not known, although climatic historians have noted that during the latter part of this period sunspot activity had decreased dramatically. The hazardous environmental situation was exacerbated by a sequence of volcanic eruptions, in southern Peru in 1600, the Philippines in 1641, and smaller volcanic episodes in 1666-1669, 1675 and 1698-99. The severe cooling effects around the world lasted for years at a time, increasing the frequency of crop failure. Bad weather bought bad harvests; bad harvests brought rural discontent and, considering the vital importance of a dispute over the harvesting of a field of oats, it is easy to see how quickly the Devil became involved. Others have speculated that bouts of agrarian madness may have been instigated by outbreaks of ergotism – hallucinogenic manias caused by the ergot mould that can grow on rye during wet seasons. Interestingly, it is possible that farmers turned to rye as a staple during this period because it is more successful in cooler climates.

THE FIELD GUIDE

Writing in 1680, Daniel Defoe summed up the paranoia endemic of the period:

*In the times of the Popish Plot, and when every day gave us new accounts
and discoveries of the hidden mysteries of that yet not completely discovered
contrivance of Hell and its agents; everybody's business you may be sure, was to
enquire "what news, what news?"*

Although it was written many years earlier, in *A Midsummer Night's Dream*
Shakespeare offers a valuable insight into the rationale behind the association of weather
with the spirit world. In the opening scene of Act 2, Puck explains that Titania and Oberon,
king and queen of the fairies, constantly argue over a changeling, a boy stolen for her by
the fairies, but craved by Oberon. Much of the play revolves around the tricks he devises,
with Puck, to steal the boy from her. As Titania explains, their quarrel has led to a break-
down in the natural world and unseasonal bad weather, and therefore to a loss of fertility
in field and fold:

*The ox hath therefore stretch'd his yoke in vain,
The ploughman lost his sweat, and the green corn
Hath rotted ere his youth attain'd a beard
...the spring, the summer,
The childing autumn, angry winter, change
Their wonted liveries, and the mazed world,
By their increase, now knows not which is which:*

Prehistory

It was not uncommon then, nor is it now, to believe that disorder in one level of the universe leads to disorder everywhere else, hence the fairies' quarrel disrupts the normal patterns of weather at the earthly level. The underlying message is that the weather will improve when the spirits are assuaged.

The Mowing Devil pamphlet also provides a taste of the harsh reality of socio-political tensions between workers and landowners in pre-industrial Britain. "Doom-saying" of the kind that reminded greedy employers that the Devil seeks retribution on behalf of oppressed workers by ruining stock was not uncommon. This manner of threat transcended class, serving as a strict warning to maintain a happy workforce. Even as late as the mid-19th century, acts of rural crime aimed at farmers and gentry, from horse theft and maiming to arson, were popularly attributed to demonic forces, giving rise to the mythical Man in Black, a dark, exotic outsider – as rural crime usually emanates close to home, the invention of a Puckish scapegoat allows communities to expel the guilt of their own ills.

Continuing our circular motif, "fairy rings" are traditionally associated with tales of unsuspecting passers-by that are lured away and, like Titania's changeling, destined to dance forever with the fairies, or to return mocked as gibbering imbeciles as they tell their story. The earliest literary reference "to the nature and efficient cause of those rings we find in the grass, which they commonly call Fairy Circles" is found in Robert Plot's *The Natural History of Staffordshire* published in 1686, just eight years after the publication of

THE FIELD GUIDE

A witch *conjures up a circle of dancing imps.*
From Nathanial Crouch's KINGDOM OF DARKNESS *(1688)*

the Mowing Devil pamphlet. Plot was a Professor of Chemistry at Oxford University and the first keeper of the city's Ashmolean museum.

While modern science may readily dismiss the idea of elves, fairies, demons and the like as nothing more than superstition, it is important to remember that in Plot's time these entities represented a view of the natural world that seemed every bit as real to people as ours does to us; strange marvels are more easily attributed to otherworldly beings if we believe they exist, and such belief was rife in 17th century Britain. Obvious problems arise in trying to separate what is natural and what is not in an environment where no such distinction was made. The morality of the time – the distinction between good and evil – dictated that what is not natural is "unnatural", with all the implications the term still carries today. To Professor Plot, however, the world he inhabited was undergoing the beginnings of a revolution in knowledge, and the ways in which it was acquired. Keeping this in mind, one of the most interesting aspects of Plot's book is that it illustrates a growing disparity between popular superstition and the truth according to Church authorities and the emergent academic institutions.

Plot interviewed witnesses and visited fairy ring sites. Getting on his hands and knees he dug into the very soil beneath the rings and tasted it. Ultimately, he favoured empiricism over mere belief, seeing through the world of nature spirits to more prosaic explanations, such as rutting deer, or hay falling from the eaves of hay-stacks, or mole dung, or even cattle urine spreading through the earth and contaminating it outwards in every direction. (Even if he did not know it, Plot found the most salient feature of our continuing engagement with mysterious phenomena, that the truth does not always lie in the most rational explanations.)

In Assen, Holland, nearly ninety years earlier in August 1590, people were spotted dancing in a circle in a field at night. We know it was a field because Plot tells how the ground they were dancing on was ploughed the following winter. The text reads:

THE FIELD GUIDE

There was found in the place where they danced a round circle wherein there were the manifest marks of the treading of cloven feet, as plain as are made by horses… [the] circle remained from the day after… till the next winter when the plow cut it out.*

It is interesting how such an account can be interpreted to suit the beliefs projected onto it, as was demonstrated at countless witch trials of the period. Rather than representing the material proof of demons, however, it could just as easily be explained as a rare sighting of circlemakers. Perhaps by a man walking his dog at midnight – the bane of present-day circlemakers. Plot goes on:

We have ample testimony from diverse sources, some of them judges who received it in confession from the criminals they condemned, all agreeing (if to be believed) that their dances were always circular… And then there are patterns not only in a single ring but sometimes in a double and treble circle, one within the other, patterns of semi-circles and quadrants and sextants of circles traced by lightening, and even meteors.

His descriptions of expanding geometry are remarkably prescient.

* *The Natural History of Staffordshire*, 1686, BY ROBERT PLOT. PLOT'S OWN SOURCE FOR THIS STORY IS *Daemonolatreia* (DEMON WORSHIPPING), 1595 BY FRENCH JUDGE AND INQUISITOR NICOLAS REMY, THE SO-CALLED "TOURQUEMADA OF LORRAINE", WHO SETS THE SCENE IN FRANCE, NOT HOLLAND. HIS BOOK WAS HAILED AS THE GREATEST ENCYCLOPÆDIA OF WITCHCRAFT SINCE *Malleus Maleficarum*.

Prehistory

Professor Plot, along with colleagues John Naylor and Hugh Todd, hypothesised that when lightning struck the ground it released sulphur into the earth, enriching the soil so that the following year the grass grew more luxuriantly. He recounts the testimony of a Mr Walker:

> *a man eminent not only for his skill in Geometry but in all other accomplishments, who by chance one day walking in a meadow amongst mowers (with whom he had been but a little before) after such a storm of lightening presently espied one of these rings about five yards diameter, with a rim about a foot broad, newly burnt bare as the colour and brittleness of the grass roots plainly testified, which the following year came more fresh and verdant in the burnt area than in the middle, and at mowing time was much taller and ranker grass than any in the meadow.*

Plot also reported other phenomena, which he believed to be meteorological in nature – "hollow tubes of lightening" and balls of light, for instance. Such a light, he recounts, was observed one night by the vicar of Wednesbury church and a couple of others as they made their way home. It was hovering stationary by the west door of the church, bright enough for them to see half a mile into what they said was an otherwise very dark night, before it suddenly blinked out.

Floating phosphorescent light phenomena of this kind have long associations

THE FIELD GUIDE

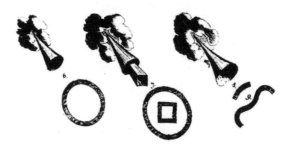

Diagrams by *Robert Plot showing the effects of wind on the ground.*

with nature spirits. The relationship is best illustrated by the names which they are known by: Will O'the Wisps, Jack O'Lanterns, *ignis fatuus* (Latin for "foolish fire", also defined as something that misleads or deludes – an illusion), fairy lights, elf lights, pixie lights, spook lights and corpse candles to name a few. Corpse candles are specifically described as small flames and are generally seen at night near churches and graveyards, as they are said to be harbingers of imminent death. Plot doesn't follow up on the fate of the vicar of Wednesbury and his friends, but presumably they lived to tell the tale. These supernatural associations also extend into modern-day study of UFOs, or Unidentified Flying Objects, and balls of light or "earthlights" as the lights tend to be known today, are frequently said to seen around crop circles.

Plot's contemporary, the antiquarian John Aubrey, also came across a similar phenomenon, which he described in his *Natural History of Wiltshire* (1686):

Prehistory

Ignis fatuus, called by the vulgar Kit of the Candlestick, is not very rare on our downes about Michaelmass.

Biding in the north lane of Broad Chalke in the harvest time in the twy-light, or scarce that, a point of light, by the hedge, expanded itselfe into a globe of about three inches diameter, or neer four, as boies blow bubbles with soape. It continued but while one could say one, two, three, or four at the most. It was about a foot from my horse's eie; and it made him turn his head quick aside from it. It was a pale light as that of a glowe-worme: it may be this is that which they call a blast or blight in the country.

We now know that fairy rings are caused by various types of fungi spreading outwards as they feed off nutrients in the soil. Sometimes the fungi are hallucinogenic – the Liberty Cap "magic" mushroom, for example, is often found on the edges of fairy rings – which may be a contributing factor to some of the associated mythology.

Of course, we are quite capable of getting carried away without the need for drugs. As Shakespeare recounts in *A Midsummer Night's Dream*, Puck and his cohorts are also influential in matters of human fertility. And there is a further reference from Agobard's writings to a letter sent to an incoming parish priest, warning that parishioners were engaging in the devilish activity of collecting seeds from flattened circles and using them in fertility rites. But could it be possible that, independently of any fairies, earth-sprites or demons, one summer evening a couple of lovers from some agrarian community made a bed in a secluded field, only for the flattened area to be interpreted later by others as evidence of something unnatural? Perhaps Bishop Agobard's warning about seeds in flattened circles has more mundane, metaphorical origins? The following posting on a crop circle website lends support to this idea:

> *We recently sold the family home, keeping most of the family's photos and documents, and I came across my granny's diary (she was born in 1871 at Monkton Farleigh, Wiltshire, near Bath). It says in there about her courting days. She says it was very difficult to find places to be alone without anybody seeing them. They would go to the cornfield and press it down with their feet, but it was always uncomfortable. She goes on to say [that] one day her husband-to-be took a thickest branch and tied to each end a piece of string and put his foot on the middle of the branch and would press the corn down in a kind of circle so they could lay down in peace and quiet with plenty of room and corn to lay on. They put several of these so-called circles in different fields, away from their houses in case they were spotted going into a field. They would not always use the same field as they could go for walks in different directions.*

> *The disturbed corn was often put down to the deer, which often made her smile, she says, as people didn't realise what they were really for. She also says in her diary she was never caught, but if she had been seen coming from them*

Prehistory

she would [have] said they went to see if there were any deer there. I am quite
sure now [that] many Wiltshire children were conceived in the corn fields of
Wiltshire, and that's where the saying comes from about a couple sowing their
seeds and having to reap the harvest. I think the moral of this story is to keep a
diary because the truth will always out. I'll always think of granny and granddad
when I pass those Farleigh cornfields. Gerry and Hollee, July 2005.

Meanwhile, a hundred miles away in rural Surrey, just a few years before Granny became a circlemaker, John Rand Capron, a Guildford solicitor and occasional scientist, was out walking in the fields near his home. That afternoon a severe storm had left the wheat fields battered – a common phenomenon known as "lodging". But Capron noticed amongst the lodged crop that there were circular marks, or "holes" as he described them, appearing from a distance. He went into the field for a closer look and made notes and a diagram. Capron sent his observations to the prestigious science journal *Nature,* to which he was a frequent contributor. The journal published the letter (alas, without the diagram) in its July 1880 issue:

> *The storms about this part of Surrey have been lately local and violent, and*
> *the effects produced in some instances curious. Visiting a neighbour's farm on*
> *Wednesday evening (21st), we found a field of standing wheat considerably*
> *knocked about, not as an entirety, but in patches forming, as viewed from a*
> *distance, circular spots.*

THE FIELD GUIDE

Examined more closely, these all presented much the same character, viz., a few standing stalks as a center, some prostrate stalks with their heads arranged pretty evenly in a direction forming a circle round the center, and outside these a circular wall of stalks which had not suffered.

I sent a sketch made on the spot, giving an idea of the most perfect of these patches. The soil is a sandy loam upon the greensand, and the crop is vigorous, with strong stems, and I could not trace locally any circumstances accounting for the peculiar forms of the patches in the field, nor indicating whether it was wind or rain, or both combined, which had caused them, beyond the general evidence everywhere of heavy rainfall. They were suggestive to me of some cyclonic wind action, and may perhaps have been noticed elsewhere by some of your readers.

Assuming that Capron had not stumbled on the site of a recent orgy, or a secret circle dance, this description adds to an emergent pattern of observations and interpretation. While his mention of "holes" may conjure Persephone's descent into the Underworld, in the absence of any scientific justification for nature spirits the circles are increasingly seen as physical trace evidence of some kind of airborne phenomenon. Capron's "cyclonic wind" is essentially too similar to Plot's torrid accounts of fiery cloudbursts and luminous hollow tubes to ignore. It was a line of enquiry that was to re-emerge exactly a century later.

Of all Capron's regular contributions to the scientific literature this one was unusual, for they mostly related to his observations through a spectroscope, which he trained on the sky at night. By curious coincidence, in Charles Fort's *Book of The Damned* (1919) the author cites Capron's published report of a torpedo-shaped "auroral beam" amongst a number of similar reports collected from the pages of science journals of the time. These UFOs were the cloud ships of the Victorian era, and the precursor by some 65 years to the arrival of flying saucers.

Between Capron's observations and the excitement surrounding an event at Evenlode in Gloucestershire, eighty years later, there are many accounts of circular ground traces – too numerous to go into individually here. They are mostly anecdotal, recalled years afterwards, perhaps in response to the recent upsurge of interest in crop circles.

What separates the Evenlode rings from the other apocrypha is the stir that they caused when reported in the *Evesham Journal* in early June 1960, attracting hundreds of visitors. The site consisted of an outer ring about seven metres in diameter with another ring inside it. The rings were thin and perfectly formed, as if, as described by a local journalist, drawn by a giant pair of compasses. The paper reported that neither the farmer nor any of his neighbours could account for the circles or recall seeing anything like them. "If there were such things as flying saucers, this is just the sort of impression one would expect them to make on landing", he said.

Grass and crop circles, and related "ground traces", had always been regarded as tangible evidence of an intervention by *something*, but by the time they were visited all we were left with was speculation. The speculation mirrored cultural preference, morphing from the ungodly, the devilish and the freakish to now being claimed by those in the know as physical evidence of visits by beings from other planets. It is understandable why mysterious circular ground markings were immediately associated with some kind of aerial phenomena, but following Capron's observations meteorology gave way to an increasing obsession for visitors from other worlds in the form of flying saucers.

Nearly a thousand years after Bishop Agobard and the Magonians, we had arrived full circle.

THE FLYING SAUCERS HAVE LANDED

The following examples are typical of reports of the post-WW2 period, at the height of saucer hysteria. In 1952, a 16ft ring of dehydrated vegetation was found in Lamont, Missouri, following multiple sightings of an unidentified flying object. Two years later a glowing object was observed touching down at La Roche-Brenil, France, leaving a 12ft ring of "ash-like" appearance. And on a May evening in 1954, Nigel Frapple was cycling home from a dance in Wincanton, Somerset, when he saw a huge illuminated metallic object, 50ft across, hovering over a field. The next day he accompanied a reporter to the scene, the Redlynch crossroads near Frapple's home in Bruton, and found "grass pushed flat in an area 100 ft in diameter, and scorched in places". While some assumed it to be the direct imprint of the belly of a craft, or its legs, or flattened by the jet thrust of landing and take-off, others saw evidence of a light-ray beamed from the craft to the ground, perhaps as a calling card?

But there is often nothing more effective at encouraging speculation than news media. In the summer of 1963, the discovery of a large crater on a farm in Charlton, Wiltshire, drew the attention of not only the local and national press, but also an emerging writer and TV personality named Patrick Moore, who published a report of his visit in *New Scientist* magazine.

The crater measured nearly eight feet across, and was situated in the middle of a potato field. Amid the general hubbub of an Army bomb disposal squad dispatched to the scene, a local policeman told reporters that the previous night he had watched as a glowing ball of orange light descended into the field. Despite the lack of fragments of any kind, official explanation settled for a meteorite that had atomised as it hit the ground.

Meanwhile, Moore was drawn beyond the perimeter of the field to something less easily explained:

> *In the adjoining wheat fields were other features taking the form of circular or elliptical areas in which the wheat had been flattened. I saw these myself; they had not been much visited, and were certainly peculiar. One, very well*

defined, was an oval, 15 yards long by 4.5 broad. There was evidence of "spiral flattening", and in one case there was a circular area in the centre of which the wheat had not been flattened. In no case was there any evidence of an actual depression in the ground.

Moore provided a fuller account ten years later in his entertaining book *Can You Speak Venusian*. It is worth repeating it here in full:

So far as I was concerned, the next highlight came in July 1963, when some peculiar craters appeared in a potato field in Charlton – not the London Charlton but a small village near Shaftsbury in Dorset. A local farmer made the discovery, and also saw the crops for a wide area around had been flattened. Reports over the radio and in the press caused widespread interest, and this was heightened by a statement from an Australian who gave his name as Robert J. Randall, from the rocket proving ground at Woomera. Dr. Randall maintained that the crater had been produced by the blast-off of a saucer from the planet Uranus. It was independently suggested that there might be a bomb in the crater, and an Army disposal team was brought in.

When the whole affair started to look really interesting, I happened to be in a television studio. We decided that whatever had happened, we ought to be "in on it". At the dead of night we drove to Charlton, and arrived in the early

Prehistory

hours to find all sorts of people hopping around about like agitated sparrows. The bomb disposal squad was at work, but had unearthed nothing but a piece of metal, which might have been anything. As I was once involved with dismembering bombs (as a passing phase during the war, while I was with the RAF), I was called in, and I had no qualms, because I thought that the chances of there being a buried explosive there were about a million to one against. There was also a dowser, marching about with an impressive assortment of twigs; there were a couple of astrologers, at least one telepath, and various local Saucerers (or Ufologists). The teeming populace was kept away by improvised fences, though I was privileged to go where I liked. The crater was evident enough. It looked as though it had been caused by subsidence, but more than that I could not really say.

We then tried to locate Dr. Randall, but could find only a relative of his who seemed to be a local nurse. Strangely, Woomera disclaimed all knowledge of anyone named Randall; we went so far as to telephone them. So far as I know, nobody has seen him since. (I can add only that he did produce a report on the Charlton affair, saying that on another occasion he had come across a grounded Uranian Saucer and had had a long conversation with the pilot, a gentleman who rejoiced in the name of Ce-fn-x.)

I did track down the rumour that when the spacecraft had landed, it had killed a cow. What had happened was that in a discussion at a local pub, a farmer had said "Ah! And, you know, a cow of mine died last week, too!" with the inevitable result that a journalist overheard, and another sensational headline was dispatched to a newspaper.

By the 1960s, America's fascination with flying saucers had spread worldwide, generated through magazines, propagandist news stories (the saucers were the perfect disguise to mask "black" weapons projects and secret aircraft), and a rash of television shows and Hollywood movies. It lasted in strength for nearly 30 years and defined our perception of the circles phenomenon during that period.

Such visions tend to reflect a canonical bias, formed from ideas that adapt and change according to our yearnings – smooth, gleaming flying saucers represented the popular notion of what the future *should* look like. Thus, the Space Age reignited an inherent spirituality; with Russian and American space programmes out of most people's reach, the saucer craze offered a unique transcendence from our earthly bonds.

The best-known UFO-related ground-trace incident occurred near the town of Tully, Queensland, Australia, in 1966. At around 9 o'clock on a warm January morning in the middle of an antipodean summer, George Pedley, a 28-year-old farm worker, was driving his tractor towards a stretch of water known locally as the Horseshoe Lagoon, which curled around an area of trees and thick scrubland. As he reached 75ft away he heard a hissing noise, so loud that it drowned out the sound of his tractor. Just as he was looking at his tyres to see if any had burst he caught sight of an object rising above the treetops. Pedley described it as large, grey and saucer-shaped, convex on the top and bottom, about as big as a bus, and it was spinning rapidly. Then, 20ft above him the object suddenly tipped its edge and zoomed off into the clear blue sky, climbing faster than an aeroplane, the hissing sound tailing off as it disappeared in the distance. Pedley reckoned that the whole encounter lasted little more than 30 seconds.

When Pedley looked on the other side of the trees, where the lagoon was normally thick with reeds he saw a bare patch, 30ft across. The object had apparently caused this as it took off because the water was still rotating. Returning three hours later, Pedley saw that the same area of water was now filled with reeds, clearly swirled in a clockwise direction and floating freely on the surface, as if each plant had been ripped from its roots. The air around him had a faint smell of sulphur.

A photo of the swirled reeds (*opposite*) taken that same afternoon by landowner Albert Pennisi, has become almost as iconic an image to researchers as the Mowing Devil woodcut. Perhaps because of this, the Tully circle is widely assumed to be a one-off event. In fact, Queensland was well known at the time for its waves of UFO sightings and the curious "nests" that were apparently left behind in reeds and cane fields, and this was one in a series of similar events in that area, ranging over a number of years. According to Pennisi, quoted in 1990, in the years following Pedley's encounter there were 22 nests

THE FIELD GUIDE

The swirled reeds of the Tully, Austrlia "saucer nest", 1966.

on the same lagoon. Interesting as it is, the encounter would have been recorded as just another anecdotal story were it not for the conjunctive "nest phenomena" – at last, here was tangible, first-hand evidence connecting one phenomenon with the other.

Mysterious flying objects are not the sole domain of ufologists, of course, for such phenomena were already firmly embedded in local folklore. Were Pedley's object witnessed by a local aborigine it would probably have been recognised as a *Chic-ah-Bunnah* or "devil man", an ancestral spirit that manifests as balls of light. As the name suggests, to the indigenous population these carry similarly morbid associations as the corpse candle and other luminosities mentioned earlier – likewise, according to local legend, to get caught by one means certain death.

Prehistory

Perhaps understandably, scientists and representatives of the Royal Australian Air Force (RAAF) who made enquiries into Pedley's story interpreted things differently. Tully is officially recognised as Australia's wettest town, and at this time of year, the wet season approaching, conditions in this part of tropical Queensland are known to attract another kind of devil, akin to dust devils and mini-tornadoes… a whirlwind known locally as the Willy Nilly. And this is how the authorities classified Pedley's object. Furthermore, the initial police report stated that a local resident named Wallace Evans had come forward with information about similar markings nearby, that he was certain were caused by whirlwinds uprooting the plants and laying them out radially. Saucer protagonists dispute this, however. For one thing, they say, it was an otherwise calm day, not the kind of weather usually associated with whirlwinds. And Pedley himself is on record as saying, "I've seen wet whirlwinds and dust whirlwinds. If the police believe this, let them. I know what I saw. It wasn't a whirlwind." Two more similar nests were found the day after. These were smaller, resting a few feet apart but only yards from the one on Horseshoe Lagoon. One of the circles was flattened in a clockwise rotation and the other counterclockwise. A week later, more were found that were believed to predate Pedley's discovery.

In the fascinating way that previously unseen phenomena emerge simultaneously in more than one place, at the same time as the Tully "nests" appeared, more examples – now in grass, oats, wheat and thistles – were being discovered across Australia and in Europe. For example, in one field in South Australia seven tightly swirled circles were found scattered over 20 acres. These were photographed at the time and the pictures appeared in the local newspaper. In the Canadian province of Saskatchewan, circles have appeared since they were first noted in the early 1970s, when a farmer encountered five "domed, metallic objects" that took off leaving five rings in grass, and later two more, making up a neat semi-circular pattern of rings.

At around the same time, similar arrangements were found at Zurich Cantone, in Switzerland, on the farm where Billy Meier lived. Meier's claim to fame is a series of close encounters with beings from the Pleiades star cluster. They made frequent visits to the farm over a period of months, arriving in gleaming, saucer-shaped craft that Meier was allowed to film at will. This is unusual, as UFOs are by their very nature defined by fleeting appearances. But these hung around – quite literally, say sceptics – long enough for Meier to make a series of films and still images, building a cult following on the strength of them. The "nests" at Zurich Cantone mainly appeared in grass and weeds, and sometimes formed in triplicate with the circles positioned in a close equilateral triangle. They were neatly swirled, always counterclockwise. Meier claimed to have seen them being made by the saucers – he describes them as "tracks" – but while he was easily able to film the saucers in flight, alas, the moment of their mark-making went unrecorded, although he did manage to capture the results in a photograph.

Prehistory

WARMINSTER

The Thing from out of Warminster
Came to the Minster school...   Children's song. c.1966

The Devil, according to local folklore, once left his tracks between Warminster, a quiet Wiltshire market town near the Somerset border, and Devizes, some 20 miles to the east. He was making his way to bury alive the townsfolk of Marlborough, but dropped his load prematurely, near Avebury, at the place now known as Silbury Hill. Whatever the historical facts behind the myth, it turned out to be prescient too.

The Warminster UFO flap ran more or less concurrently with Tully's. It all began rather benignly in the spring of 1964 with a sound. A witness claimed that several birds were disturbed by the noise, but they then keeled over and died. Nearly eight months later, on Christmas morning, the local postmaster was woken by a noise on his roof. It sounded, he said, as if the tiles were being ripped off with tremendous force. He added that it then sounded like they were slammed back into place, and presumably the physical evidence supported that. Another witness who lived nearby heard a droning sound, and sensed that it was causing vibration. Her dog was found hiding in the garden shed. Subsequent accounts include a man whose head was apparently caught up in some kind of pressure wave and shaken violently from side to side, until it was just as sharply released. And on an otherwise still summer's evening in 1965, three children playing beside a stream were suddenly swept over and pinned to the ground by an invisible force.

THE FIELD GUIDE

There are few real mysteries in a place like Warminster, especially as loud and public as these, and the local reporter from the *Warminster Times* made the most of it. Arthur Shuttlewood interviewed witnesses and gathered opinion on the High Street, and the more opinion he gathered and reported, the bigger the mystery became. It was perhaps inevitable then, that sooner or later it would manifest as something more tangible.

In his *A Natural History of Wiltshire*, John Aubrey – who first identified the prehistoric earthworks at Avebury as a vast temple complex – reported a "fireball in the sky" over Warminster. Others had seen similar lights, usually at dusk whilst out walking on the secluded hills that surround the town – the view from Cley Hill lasts for miles in every direction, past the Westbury white horse and on to the southern reaches of the Cotswolds in one direction, across the military ranges of Salisbury Plain in the other. Shuttlewood made the connection between the lights and the sounds, and following his lead the community's attention turned to the skies. Much too diligent a journalist to indulge in further fancy, given the scarcity of facts, Shuttlewood opted to describe whatever the causal phenomena was as, simply, The Thing... The Warminster Thing.

Hordes of mystery seekers, flying saucer enthusiasts and the just-curious filled their flasks, packed their waterproofs and followed Shuttlewood to the hills for nightly sky-watches. The lights were usually a subtle amber colour, with occasional shifts to pink. While some people reported "cigar-shaped" lights, mainly they were spherical – these came to be known as "amber gambolers" due to their apparent tendency to float horizontally. They

Prehistory

Arthur Shuttlewood *(background) with the Marquis of Bath; Shuttlewood's first book.*

were too close to be stars or planets, advised Shuttlewood, and much too slow-moving to be aircraft. And other times they appeared stationary, just hanging over the town, as if waiting for something – whatever it was, The Thing appeared to be sentient and purposeful. The thing about The Thing is that it was never the same thing; it was never predictable.

In August 1965 the District Council held a public meeting to discuss the mystery and its implications to the town. Apart from the council leader, the panel consisted of UFO experts and a local priest with an interest in astronomy. More than 500 people attended, including many reporters from the national press and TV news. Consequently, the following holiday weekend saw 10,000 visitors to Warminster. It was the first time since the end of WW2 that the town's pubs had run dry. Whatever The Thing was, it was certainly good for business.

But behind the journalistic façade and his tantalising euphemism, Shuttlewood held few doubts that aliens from Outer Space were visiting Warminster. Easing into his role at the forefront of paranormal research, over the following decade he wrote a number of books and magazine articles on the subject, as well as their purpose and influence regarding the approaching New Age. In his first book, *The Warminster Mystery,* Shuttlewood describes how in January 1966 – curiously, within days of the famous Tully event – he and Lord Bath, resident of Longleat House and its vast estate outside Warminster, investigated several areas of flattened reeds on a lake nearby. He also saw similar effects in grass. As far as Shuttlewood was concerned, they were "landing spots", and like the Tully nest were swirled clockwise, their "blades swept smoothly inert in shallow depressions".

Shuttlewood's 1971 book *UFOs, Key to the New Age* features a frontispiece with four photographs showing flattened areas of numerous shapes and sizes but displaying an apparently deliberate geometry, found in local wheat fields. And in August 1972, Shuttlewood and American journalist Bryce Bond claimed to have observed the creation of a circle at Star Hill, just outside Warminster – it looked, they said, "like a lady opening a fan". Other circles were found nearby.

It is probably fair to say that people who gather together to witness UFOs share a common belief that what they are seeing is not easily explained. While it may be obvious to casual observers that stars, orbiting satellites or flares from a distant army range are not alien spacecraft, and that the large luminous globe you see in the rear view mirror as you drive along a country road at night is not actually chasing the car, it is the moon, this is not the case for everyone.

Many ufologists tend to start with the presumption that such objects are uniquely mysterious, probably spaceships, and only reluctantly accept evidence to the contrary, if at all. From this elevated standpoint, reports of direct one-to-one interaction between viewer and the viewed has emerged as a common motif in UFO accounts: an overwhelming sense that the UFO, or a corpse candle or *Chic-ah-Bunnah,* is somehow responding to *us,* to *our* thoughts and actions. This kind of interpretative response displays a typical Gestaltist disposition to impose order, in this case "intelligent" behaviour, on whatever we see. (For those who favour exotic explanations, of course, it is the nay-sayers who impose order.)

If centre stage to Shuttlewood's *son et lumière* was taken by various manifestations of The Thing, waiting in the wings were a host of bit-part invisibilities. For example, the Invisible Walker, easily identified by the sound of footsteps in the dark, and occasional "cough-like" noises heard around the hilltops; the "Aenstrian" spacemen who took to telephoning Shuttlewood and visiting him when no-one else was around. Accordingly, the beings were human but more evolved than the rest of us. When they were not passing messages of "great import" to Shuttlewood, they developed a habit of hurling themselves in front of cars on lonely roads around Warminster, only to vanish when the cars stopped. And then there was the vanished livestock: speculation became rife that the same government spooks and debunkers that destroyed the saucer nests, suppressed other UFO evidence and ridiculed honest believers, had mutilated hundreds of farm animals and then hidden them from view.

One creature that Shuttlewood describes in his 1979 book *More UFOs Over Warminster* returned 10 years later in crop circles folklore. Although it was never actually seen by researchers it made itself known by "the two-noted trilling of what has been termed the Tin-throated or Mechanical Bird, stereophonic and all about surprised sky-watchers, no naturalist or bird-lover able to identify the ear piercing warble of the unseen cosmic songster... Are the warbling mechanical bird, the heavy stepping Invisible Walker and the crackling serpent all unearthly derivatives from the same source?" asked Shuttlewood. "And do they all tie up with our worldwide UFO mystery?"

59

Warminster's status as a UFO hotspot was now assured but, alas, by the mid-1970s the party had run its course for all but a few die-hards. David Kingston was one, his resilience still evident as he continues to promote the mysteries of his native West Country. His internet article *The History of Crop Circles* * describes how during the summer of 1976 he and a group of sky-watchers were on top of Cley Hill, when three amber orbs of light began weaving around and between them. Suddenly, one of the orbs swooped down the side of the hill and vanished into the darkness. As dawn broke, Kingston noticed a flattened circle in a wheat field, at about the same spot the orb had disappeared. It was 30 feet in diameter, he writes, and perfectly swirled.

* HTTP://WWW.THEMYSTICA.COM/MYSTICA/ARTICLES/H/HISTORY_OF_CROP_CIRCLES_THE.HTML

WHAT DO YOU THINK WOULD HAPPEN IF WE PUT ONE OVER THERE?

THE FIELD GUIDE

One Friday evening in the summer of 1976, two friends from Southampton, Doug Bower and Dave Chorley, were out for their weekly get-together at the Percy Hobbs pub at Cheesefoot Head, near Winchester, about 50 miles east of Warminster. Before driving home, they decided to take a stroll, to get some air and walk off some of the beer, so they wandered along a bridle path that bounds the wheat fields on the Longwood Estate. On the other side of the path is a steep slope down to the Devil's Punchbowl, a natural amphitheatre that is now, most years, also used to grow cereals. Thirty-two summers earlier, General Eisenhower had used its slopes to address American troops on the eve of the D-Day invasion. But now the only things standing to attention in the surrounding fields were a phalanx of wheat stalks, neatly drilled by retired Lt-Commander Henry Bruce, the farmer.

Doug and Dave's conversation frequently turned to the subject of UFOs – it was mainly Doug's interest, but Dave was always happy to go along with it – and tonight was no different. Like thousands of boys growing up in the late 1940s, Doug Bower was captivated by stories of flying saucers and visitors from other worlds. While he didn't exactly believe everything he read, one senses from meeting Doug that the transcendental spirit of UFO mythology had made a formative impression that had never quite left him. The two men talked about Shuttlewood's books, and the lights and sounds and the "saucer nests" seen at Warminster. Then Doug was reminded of similar news stories he had read when he and his wife had lived in Melbourne, Australia, in the mid-sixties. He told Dave about the sighting at Tully of a flying saucer and the nest it had left. Then Doug Bower

The Beginning

uttered the words that would herald a new era in the history of crop circles: "What do you think would happen if we put one over there?" he asked Dave casually, pointing at the sea of wheat beside them, "People would think a flying saucer had landed." Dave liked the idea, and before they knew it the idea had hatched into a fledgling plan.

Doug Bower, *foreground, and Dave Chorley creating a portal to other worlds.*

THE FIELD GUIDE

The following Friday, when they went out for a drink they took a bar with them, the sturdy metal bar that normally secured the back door to Doug's framing shop and art studio. Now it doubled as an ideal tool for flattening wheat plants. After an extra drink to steady their nerves, as the evening light faded the two men set off along the bridle path and, once they were sure they were not being observed, slipped stealthily into the field. Somewhere near the centre, the two men moved out of the tramline and into the virgin wheat. A few feet in they got down on their hands and knees and, using one end of the bar as a pivot, flattened a swathe of wheat into a small circle. Each holding one end of the bar, they then pushed their way around the edge of the circle, extending the circumference with each circuit. With every full rotation the circles get bigger of course, and after about half-an-hour they were too tired and sore-kneed to continue. A diameter of 30ft seemed plenty, though – after all, they were only mimicking the nests Doug had read about in his UFO books, and any larger might seem unrealistic. But even if the circle was quite small compared to what was to come, the biggest and most lasting impression they made that night was the shared sense of artistic pride.

Art ultimately requires an audience though, and as far as Doug and Dave knew, that first circle went completely unnoticed. If the fruits of their nocturnal labours had impressed the likes of David Kingston and his fellow Warminster watchers, Doug and Dave were far too detached from things to hear of it – such was the lot of anonymous artists before the spread of the Internet.

The Beginning

It was not until August 1980, after nearly five summers of Doug and Dave's weekly efforts, that the crop circles made their dramatic re-entry into popular awareness, through a headline in the *Wiltshire Times*.

Mystery Circles—Return Of The 'Thing'?

THE Warminster 'Thing' could be back. Speculation that the UFO, which hundreds of people claimed to have seen in the mid and late 1960s, began again this week after three circular depressions appeared in cornfields near Westbury White Horse.

The depressions have mystified local farmers and tourists to the White Horse and the Army could come up with no immediate explanation.

Two of the marks, which are perfect circles about 18 yards across, are clearly visible in a

MYSTERY CIRCLES – RETURN OF THE THING?

The Warminster "Thing" could be back. Speculation that the UFO, which hundreds of people claimed to have seen in the mid and late 1960s, began again this week after three circular depressions appeared in cornfields near Westbury White Horse.

THE FIELD GUIDE

The article went on to describe the clockwise swirls and the absence of tracks. The latter was the earliest indicator that humans could not be responsible for the formations. And besides, the circles looked much too well defined and regular, beautiful even, to be the work of jokers. The army was mystified, denying that the tightly-swirled lay of the crop could have been caused by the downwash of helicopter blades. Nor could weather have been responsible, according to a local farmer, who told the paper "I have never seen marks like it before. It certainly cannot be wind or rain damage, because I have seen plenty of that and it is just not that regular. If it's not a helicopter, then it is very mysterious."

The three circles had in fact appeared over a period of months, between May and July, and in two different fields.

Until he was called in to investigate the Westbury circles, Dr Terence Meaden had remained oblivious to the supernatural goings-on at Warminster, and even if he had heard or read about it, it is safe to assume that his interpretation would have differed from Shuttlewood's. So he brought with him no preconceptions, except those formed from his own considerable scientific expertise. As with Shuttlewood and the ufologists, the circles mystified him. But what separates physicists from metaphysicists is that mystery represents a challenge for science to overcome, and he soon overcame it with an explanation that fitted his expertise perfectly.

Being such a rare event, Meaden would have left it at that had it not been for the

The Beginning

arrival of three more circles the following week. They were found together in the Devil's Punchbowl, in the lee of Cheesefoot Head, thus providing further evidence for Meaden's hypothesis (which he now adapted slightly to accommodate the multiplicity of circles). If the trio ensemble marked the beginnings of an evolution in circles design, the evolution of Meaden's theory ran parallel. What were to Doug and Dave simple practicalities – three circles were more easily noticed than one, and overlooking hills made for convenient viewing – represented to Meaden confirmation of his own thinking. The three circles lay in a line, with the outer circles about 25ft diameter and the central one more than twice that size. Writing in his *Journal of Meteorology*, Dr Meaden explained the symmetry as follows:

> *Possibly, moreover, after the life and death of the first whirlwind, the*
> *frontal boundary twice advanced some 25 metres before halting and*
> *permitting the thermal to re-establish itself as a new whirlwind. We*
> *infer that the three damage patterns lay close to one another, not because*
> *of chance coincidence, but because of the special position of their site*
> *relative to the adjacent hill.*

Despite Doug and Dave's best efforts at reigniting the public's interest in flying saucers, with them at the helm, the more circles they made the more Dr Meaden – on the strength of his expertise he was soon considered the leading authority on the subject – was able to explain them away by natural causes. If in Doug Bower's mind it was

Three circles *appeared near Westbury in 1980.*

The last to arrive (top), in wheat, in August, was featured in the WILTSHIRE TIMES, *and attracted the attention of the first crop circles researchers, including Dr Terence Meaden.*

By this time the earlier barley circle had been harvested, but it can be seen here (bottom) in Doug Bower's photo taken as the combine harvesters close in. Its location was subsequently confirmed by the farmer.

The image is evidence that Doug & Dave's involvement preceded the media interest and any subsequent crop circles research.

obvious that a quintuplet arrangement of four circles surrounding a larger central circle suggested a four-legged spaceship had landed, Meaden remained oblivious to any such artful symbolism. As the physicist Richard Feynman observed, "a scientist looking at non-scientific problems is just as dumb as the next guy."

The symbolism was not lost on everyone, though. This is also the symbol of the *quinta essentia*, the fifth and highest element after air and earth and fire and water, believed to be the substance composing all heavenly bodies – in alchemical terms, the Philosopher's Stone. To others it resembled the mystical Celtic cross. Often, so much of the power of a symbol lies in its one-size-fits-all malleability.

As the patterns grew in size and composition, from single circles to ringed circles and circle formations, the more Meaden accommodated the facts into his theory, the more Doug and Dave worked to prove him wrong. Once, Meaden made the observation that in all the quintuplet formations the individual circles were swirled clockwise, only for the very next to feature one anticlockwise circle.

While Meaden considered the meteorological implications, symbologists pointed to a reference made by the philosopher Carl Jung in his book on flying saucers about the Christian iconography of the 3+1 structure: in the centre, God, surrounded by a Holy Trinity; the anticlockwise fourth element representing the demon Antichrist.

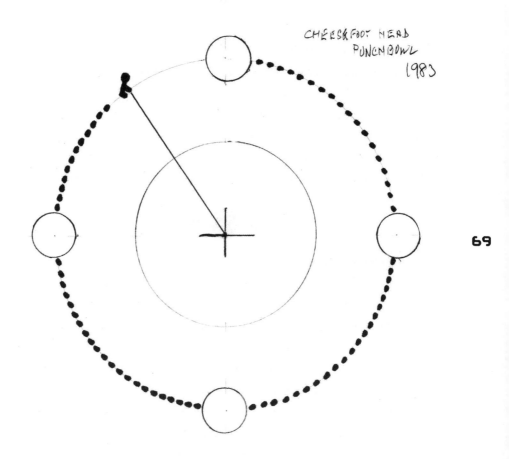

An early *Doug Bower diagram for a circle that appeared at Cheesefoot Head, 1983.*

The Beginning

The flip side to Feynman's observation, of course, is that in non-scientific research anyone can claim to be as qualified as the next guy. Symbolic or not, there was something about the quintuplet formations that screamed "intelligent design", and their arrival set off a frenzy of media speculation. In turn, predictably, this attracted a rag-tag of would-be scientists-cum-mystics jostling to challenge Meaden as the voice of authority, to be a big fish in a small pond. This was convenient as far as the news media were concerned, because they restored a kind of natural balance – now the Dr's dry, matter-of-fact and highly non-speculative explanations could be pitted against more exotic notions.

CEREALOGIA

It was not long before the latter became dominant. One of the most vocal exponents of this new science of "cerealogy" was Colin Andrews, a Technical Services Support Officer for the Test Valley Borough Council, based in Andover, Hampshire, just a short drive from Cheesefoot Head. It's important to be precise with his job title because, as his fame grew, Andrews took to describing himself as the Council's Chief Electrical Engineer, and threatened to sue anyone who said differently. As one contemporary observed, "He could not rid himself of the bumptious respectability that was associated with officialdom, what Shakespeare called 'the Bum Bailiff'". Furthermore, Andrews allowed the odd ill-briefed journalist to describe him as a scientist, and even on occasion "Professor" – with

THE FIELD GUIDE

Meaden's scientific superiority thus neutralised, any difference in their opinions of what was causing the circles would be seen as just that, two experts disagreeing over the finer points of theory. But Andrews' insecurity was tempered with intense sincerity, and listening to him it was all too easy to be swayed by his delusions. And besides this, the intensity carried with it an air of oppression, or suppression, as if Andrews was always under threat from the powers-that-be to remain quiet about what he knew. A contagious sense spread amongst his followers that he must be on to something, and in their eyes Andrews was a hero because he would not be silenced.

Colin Andrews, *centre, with research team.*

The Beginning

Pat Delgado, *left, interviewed by UFO researcher Michael Hesseman.*

By now the self-styled "world's foremost authority on crop circles", Andrews combined these energies with those of another pioneering circles researcher, Pat Delgado, and the subject immediately took off to new heights of speculative abandon. Delgado lived just a stroll away from Cheesefoot Head in the picturesque Hampshire village of Arlesford. In the early 1960s he had worked at NASA's Deep Space Tracking Range at Woomera, south Australia. Although only maintaining the antennae there, it is very possible that he came into contact with Mr Randall, the Uranus buff who took such an interest in the Charlton crater at that time. If he had, Delgado never mentioned it. Now retired, he spent most summer days driving around the area on the lookout for new circles. When

THE FIELD GUIDE

Doug Bower *working on diagrams outside the Percy Hobbs.*

he found them he would immediately telephone Andrews and, until competition became intolerable, Dr Meaden. Then, in the evenings, he would write up reports for the local press. Inevitably, however, they tended toward the over-technical, and more often than not ended up being published in the *Flying Saucer Review*. Even though the old "saucer nests" were lost in the tide of mystical symbolism and emergent questions of divine communication, the ideal of the landed spacecraft had not diminished entirely.

This pleased Doug Bower no end. There was nothing he enjoyed more than to go along to the Percy Hobbs pub and join in the meetings held in honour of Andrews

The Beginning

and Delgado, themselves frequent visitors, listening to the talk about measurements and placement; how so-and-so had used dowsing rods to determine the strength of the energy lines running through the circles, and how incredibly strong they were; and what this all meant in relation to the symbolism. More than anything, though, Doug and Dave's biggest laughs – barely stifled until they reached the safety of the car for the ride home – were had at the seriousness with which the experts referred to the "superior intelligences" behind the circles.

Meanwhile, Lt-Commander Bruce, who farmed the Devil's Punchbowl, took an understandably different stance. He told the *Southern Evening Echo* that the circles were the work of "grown-up children". "People who grow up with fairy tales always believe them," he complained. "I would not even contemplate UFOs... they know perfectly well it's not true."

By this time, Andrews and Delgado had secured a three-book deal with a major publisher and the first, *Circular Evidence,* had become a best-seller. The pair were now celebrities. At press conferences, reporters were not particularly bothered that they could never quite say with certainty what was making the circles. In contrast to Meaden, Andrews and Delgado had learned that the key to success in the business of non-science lies in not finding answers, and offered variations on the theme of "we're working on it". On the whole, the news media seemed perfectly content with this, because in the absence of an answer it meant that they could tell the same story over and over again.

Michael Green, *first Chairman of the CCCS.*

Reading between the lines of this perpetual ambiguity it was easy to see where their sympathies lay, however. While Andrews liked to say that the circles were formed "by an unknown intelligence by an unknown force in an unknown manner", Delgado's view differed slightly. For him, the more senior engineer/scientist of the two, an "IUFF", or Invisible Unknown Force Field, must be involved. Even Dr Meaden couldn't disagree.

With Andrews and Delgado's research made unavailable to them (except through their books), it wasn't long before other investigators decided to organise into an official research body that the media and public would respect. Then they could publish

The Beginning

their own books. In 1989, the Centre for Crop Circles Studies (CCCS) was formed, with a fitting ceremony at the top of Silbury Hill, led by its first chairman Michael Green. Green summoned the spirit guardian of the hill to commune with the spirit of the circles that were now appearing in the immediate area, right below the hill. "We know the guardian responded because someone was recording the ceremony and you can hear a droning sound on the tape", said Green. "That was a distant airplane!" said another who was there.

Besides Green, the CCCS was fronted by Professor Archie Roy BSc, PhD, FRAS, FRSE, FBIS (President), who had followed Rita Goold into circles research, and John, Earl of Haddington (Founder), a likable peer with big eyes for nature spirits. Further down the ladder was George Wingfield (Field Officer), Haddington's old school chum from Eton and Trinity College, Dublin, who worked as a systems analyst for IBM.

Conferences and symposiums were arranged and well attended. The most popular was held each year in Glastonbury – The Glastonbury Cornference, organised by John Michell, an Eton-educated author of many books on Sacred Geometry and editor of *The Cerealogist*, the magazine of choice for circles connoisseurs – with two days of speakers and slideshows of the latest circles, ending with a mass meditation in the nearby abbey ruins.

It took someone with an appreciation of the workings of government to see through the charade and to want to expose it. Writing in the *Daily Telegraph*, Matt Ridley, the son of a Cabinet minister, explained that "the chief believers appeal to people's love of mystery by saying the phenomenon lies outside conventional science, and then promptly assuage the media's thirst for bogus expertise. They form committees, hold conferences, and parade their credentials."

Few paid any attention. It was much more than a middle-class mafia, it was theatrical as well. And if the Eton luvvies didn't exactly kick off a class war with the CCCS membership (numbering 1000 at its height) there was enough deference from the lesser ranks of circles spotters, measurers, local group secretaries and enterprising conference organisers to feed this higher echelon of high-minded antiquarians, alien language linguists, symbologists, mythologists and so on down the parade.

Meanwhile, Dr Meaden cut a lonely figure in comparison. While, privately, he held a seething contempt for the CCCS and tried to distance himself and his ideas from what he saw as its occultist following, he was not entirely immune from its influence. The popularity of the circles meant a constant influx of raw data, and like any good scientist Meaden was hungry to refine his theory by accommodating it. The problem was that this tended to run one way and not the other, with Meaden absorbing more into his theory than he rejected, even if it was clear to others that the information was unreliable.

The Beginning

The tale of the South Seas islanders unable to see Captain Cook's ship because they had never seen anything so vast might be apocryphal but it reflects a real truth; perception is shaped by the local and cultural environment. Outside the "correct" context, our experiences are no longer governed by familiar or given conditions. This blindness is a cognitive dissonance.

There are some people who are educated far beyond their ability to see the obvious, and it is perhaps characteristic of the naïvely honest academic within Dr Meaden that he failed to notice a "trout in the milk" – clear circumstantial evidence of suspicious human manufacture – as it unfolded before him. In this, he made the same mistake as the "cranks" he despised, basing his judgements on false premise and opinion rather than the evidence itself.

First, there was the dramatic rise in numbers. In less than a decade, sporadic circles here and there had increased to hundreds per season, in specific localised areas: In 1987 Meaden recorded a total of 73 circles; in 1988, 113; in 1989, 308 – over 80 in the Silbury Hill area alone; and during the summer of 1990 more than 700 circles were committed to the database of his Circles Effect Research Unit (CERES). It is important to note that these figures represent individual circles, even when they were part of a larger formation – ie a quincunx consisting of five circles was recorded as five individual circles, rather than a single event. While no researcher has fully explained the reasons for this – to Meaden, it was probably a matter of scientific protocol – some observers suspected that the sheer volume of circles encouraged us to assume that the phenomenon as a whole was well beyond human capabilities, and that by separating the circles, attention was drawn away from the undeniable, ever-evolving geometrical symbolism.

Another example is the obvious difference between the kind of whirlwinds Meaden was describing in the halcyon years – one commonly associated with warm daytime conditions – and the glaring fact that the circles arrived during the hours of darkness. Rather than properly addressing all the possible reasons for the disparity he simply expanded the capability of his vortex model. That is not to say that his colleagues hadn't warned him; Paul Fuller, for instance, a ufologist who initially supported Meaden's ideas, was growing increasingly suspicious that they accounted for only a proportion of what was really going on.

Dr Meaden had by this time acquainted himself with the mythic associations of crop circles and UFOs. There were so many shared commonalities within historical accounts and the current circles-related experiences being reported to him that he began to think that his theory could explain these too. For Arthur Shuttlewood's story of how he witnessed a circle forming, accompanied by a high-pitched humming noise, Meaden had the answer: "The fast-spinning vortices are also known to emit a humming noise", he claimed. Furthermore, "it is because of the electrical effects accompanying these vortices that night-time events are sometimes, perhaps often, luminous." How likely was it that this could account for the lights over Warminster? Was The Thing actually an atmospheric vortex? And what about the countless ground trace cases with accompanying light phenomena? Or balls of light?

It then occurred to Meaden that there was an abundance of experiences associated with UFO sightings – car stops, exhausted batteries, even accounts of so-called "alien abduction", a pastime then in its infancy – that could be satisfactorily explained by his theory. Likewise, the Mowing Devil. As Meaden wrote: "The seventeenth century publisher's illustration of the devil at work leaves little doubt that these were the result of spiralling vortices". For "devil", said Meaden, consider its etymological association with the Sanskrit "devi" or "goddess" – for in their proximity to sacred sites he was beginning to see in the crop circles a far bigger picture; they were the offspring of Mother Earth, issued via a giant atmospheric birth canal, a symbol of all Her powers of regeneration.

Furthermore, weren't many of the patterns found in the fields replicated on ancient megaliths, such as the "cup and ring" carvings at Long Meg and Her Daughters in Cumbria? It was only a relatively short step from here for Meaden to posit that ancient stone circles were erected to mark the places where crop circles had landed thousands of years ago: "Neolithic people could well have fancied the spiral circles to be the work and signs of passing spirits issuing from the womb of the Great Goddess", he wrote. It was as if Meaden's ideas had taken on the extraordinary breadth of a Universal Theory of Everything Remotely Unusual or Supernatural (UTERUS).

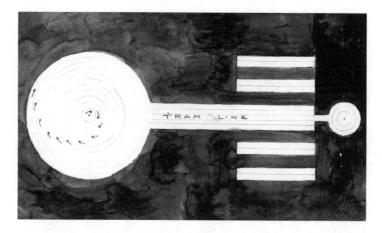

Doug Bower's *diagram of the first pictogram.*

While Doug and Dave could somehow relate to Andrews and Delgado and the church of CCCS, even if their take on the circles was a little esoteric at times (to say the least), Meaden irritated them. Each time they falsified one of his predictions about the behaviour of the circles, he sidestepped them. What they wanted was for someone to admit that they'd been wrong. Anyone! Or perhaps the pair subconsciously desired some credit for all they had done for the last fifteen years. After all, they had created a body of work that any artist would be proud of, even if it only lived by anonymity.

Pat Delgado *photographing the second pictogram.*

A RUSSIAN REVOLUTION

In May 1990, Doug and Dave decided to create a crop pattern that no plasma vortex could ever make. The addition of straight lines would demonstrate that crop circles are not made by weather. The first linear "pictogram"* duly appeared in a field of young wheat at Chilcomb, south of Cheesefoot Head. It consisted of two circles – one 40ft in diameter, the other 10ft – linked by an avenue of flattened crop. This was separated from

---

* THE WORD "PICTOGRAM" WAS ASSIGNED BY DELGADO, UNDER ADVICE FROM THE BRITISH MUSEUM. "AGRIGLYPH" WAS ALSO POPULAR.

the smaller circle by a thin wall of standing wheat. Running parallel to the avenue, mid-way there were four narrow rectangles, or "boxes" – two on each side, neatly equidistant. These were each approximately four feet wide, about the length of the wooden planks the pair used – now one each – instead of the metal security bar they once shared. Halfway down the avenue it suddenly narrowed by half, at an imaginary intersection marking one end of the four boxes. The idea for this revolutionary advance in design had come to the pair as they leafed through one of Doug's art books, a chapter on Russian Constructivism featuring the likes of Malevich, Lissitsky and Rodchenko, and specifically a work entitled "Young Woman" by George Ribemont-Dessaignes.

Doug and Dave followed this up with another, similar in design except that the larger of the two circles was surrounded by a ring, four feet wide. A few miles away, on another night they made a large ring surrounding a circle. Between the circle and the ring were four concentric arcs, symmetrically offset. It looked like a logo for an audio equipment manufacturer, or some kind of Chinese symbol – that was the thing about the pictograms; it was hard to tell what they were supposed to mean, if anything.

By now it was obvious to Doug and Dave that they were not the only ones making circles. Whilst their favoured stomping ground of Hampshire and the Wiltshire borders remained otherwise relatively untouched, for the past few years their patterns had been mirrored in the vast cereal fields surrounding Avebury and Silbury Hill, about 30 miles northwest of Cheesefoot Head. Their invention had taken on a life of its own.

The Beginning

What's more, the north Wiltshire circles were bigger than theirs. And so it was that on the morning of Thursday, 12th July 1990, Doug and Dave were left behind forever as the first of the "double-pictograms" appeared in the East Field at Alton Barnes. Like the Devil's Punchbowl, the East Field is situated below an arc of steep hills, with an overlooking road, and likewise it makes an ideal amphitheatre for circles spotting. Henceforth it became known to circlemakers as "Ground Zero".

The double pictogram would prove a defining moment in crop circle history, escalating the phenomenon in scale and complexity and being deemed epic enough to be used on the cover of Led Zeppelin's greatest hits collection. The phenomenon was about to enter a spectacular new phase.

East Field *double pictogram, 1990.*

THE STAKES ARE RAISED

The arrival of the pictograms, with the suggestion of a guiding intelligence that they implicitly contained, galvanised the circles community into increasingly dramatic action. Within days of the East Field pictogram's appearance, Colin Andrews' Operation Blackbird was underway. This was his second attempt to capture the elusive circle-making agency on video, following Operation White Crow at Cheesefoot Head the previous year, whose cameras had recorded little of interest, possibly because they were pointing at a field of peas. Andrews, the world's media hanging on his every word, was ready to settle the mystery once and for all.

For the current operation, following the huge success of their book, Andrews and Delgado enjoyed the technical support of two television companies, the BBC and Nippon TV. In addition, the British Army provided liaison support, as the site, at Bratton Castle, bordered a live firing range.

85

Bratton Castle, the remains of an ancient hill fort, is situated on top of White Horse Hill, so called because the image of a white horse is carved into the escarpment and is visible for miles around. It overlooks the Wiltshire town of Westbury, a concrete factory on its outskirts – a permanent plume of smoke belching from a solitary chimney makes it a recognised landmark – and a flat expanse of farmland stretching to the county town of Trowbridge, five miles away. At the foot of the hill, under the watchful gaze of various low-light cameras and thermal-imaging equipment provided by the TV companies, a patchwork of wheat fields formed a vast virgin canvas that would tempt any adventurous artist.

Rather than the exaggerated Army presence that Andrews claimed, in reality

The Beginning

the site was manned by various unpaid volunteers, mostly teenagers with time to spare. Time, and an unquenchable passion for crop circles. These included lads from Delgado's home village of Arlesford, and a group of friends, mainly from Trowbridge, known collectively as UBI.

Ostensibly, this stood for United Bureau of Investigation, and they had business cards printed to prove it, but privately its members said it meant United Believers in Intelligence – an intelligence beyond this planet, but manifesting itself occasionally in UFOs and crop circles. At least one of the members was an "alien abductee", claiming that aliens had subconsciously directed him to the site of Operation Blackbird, like a moth to a flame.

UBI's "Philosophical Director" was John Martineau, a young, but much-liked and respected circles researcher with an interest in geometry and, incidentally, like fellow researchers George Wingfield, John Michell and Lord Haddington, another old Etonian. It would be another couple of years before UBI's own circle-making activities were revealed.

In the relatively small community of hard-core crop circles enthusiasts, UBI formed part of an extended, informal network of friends and confidants. As Alton Barnes became a magnet for circlemakers and circles seekers alike, some of these associates took to camping in a caravan at the edge of the East Field, courtesy of the farmer's wife Polly Carson, who had arranged for the space to be cleared to accommodate the hordes of visitors.

UBI's *Paul, Bart and Matt.*

These dreadlocked campers had free access to the fields at night, ostensibly "guarding them from hoaxers". In this, there was probably less connivance on Polly's part than blindness to what she didn't want to know. Her belief that the circles arriving on her land in such numbers was no accident was much too strong to be dissuaded by mere rumours of human mischief. On the other side of the field was another, smaller caravan. Out of this were sold T-shirts and key rings with pictures of the latest circles designs. UBI helped with subsequent watches too, which in following years usually centred around the East Field.

The Beginning

Whether UBI or its associates made the "double pictogram" will perhaps never be known for certain. While they claimed such events as "genuine", they said the same of others which they would later admit to making. The apparent paradox, of course, is that UBI and others following in Bower and Chorley's footsteps, claimed to believe that crop circles are the work of a higher intelligence, and yet they still felt the need to go out into the fields and make their own.

UBI reasoned that if an alien intelligence can communicate to them by symbolism, they should be able to address it in turn, in the same ecstatic language, thereby establishing a dialogue. Viewed this way, their activities are probably best described as an elaborate devotional exchange rather than "hoaxing". But the concept of human circlemaking was, just as it is today, regarded by croppies not only as an immoral, costly distraction from the "genuine" circles, but also a poisonous disparagement of the circles phenomenon as a whole. For Andrews' trusted helpers, Operation Blackbird represented the focal point of this spiritual dialectic interface – not unlike the fictional activities at Devil's Tower mountain in Steven Spielberg's *Close Encounters of the Third Kind* – and by simply volunteering they placed themselves at centre of the action.

Other frequent visitors to the Operation Blackbird site included the artist/musicians Bill Drummond and Jim Cauty, core members of the acid-house band KLF (Kopyright Liberation Front), otherwise known as the Justified Ancients of Mu Mu. Drummond stood out especially, remember witnesses, due to his dress: a skirt, a blue suede coat and a long fake beard topped with a bowler hat.

Colin Andrews had left strict instructions with these volunteers to contact him immediately in the event of any circles appearing, and at the crack of a fine Wednesday morning the call came. As he drove to the site, Andrews called his list of media contacts, giving live interviews and arranging more. Figuring it takes around two-to-three hours to drive from London to Westbury he called a press conference for 10am. Long before that, however, as promised, Andrews granted his BBC sponsors an early exclusive, broadcast live on Breakfast News from a windy hilltop in Wiltshire:

> **Andrews:** *Well, we do have a major event here... ah, very much excitement, as you can imagine. We do have two major ground markings which appeared in front of all of the surveillance equipment, performing absolutely to form for us. We had a situation at approximately 3.30am this morning. On the monitor a number of orange lights taking the form of a triangle... It's a complex situation, and we are actually analysing it at this very moment, but there is undoubtedly something here for science.*

> **Interviewer:** *I'm sure you have the nation agog. Are you quite sure you couldn't have been the victim of some elaborate hoax last night?*

The Beginning

Andrews: *No, not indeed. We have high quality equipment here and we have indeed secured on high quality equipment a major event... We do have something of great, great significance... Yes, we have everything on film and we do have, as I say, a formed object over a field... We are doing nothing more now until we have helicopters over the top, to film in detail what we have, before anyone enters the field.*

Interviewer: *Gosh! We had better let you get on with it. We look forward to seeing the pics.*

The ringed circles – one approximately 100ft across, the other half that size – and a neat arrangement of four smaller circles and straight lines were situated in a wheat field below the hill, easily visible to the crowd of reporters that surrounded Andrews, and in full view of the cameras. Through a telescope, a volunteer noticed that there was something lying at the centre of each circle, something blue and indiscernible. But her observation was lost in the hubbub of Andrews' media moment. Somewhere in the crowd was a man in a skirt. The man from *The Times* described the atmosphere as one of "silly season gaiety", as "Mr Andrews spoke of 'an airborne consciousness', which he declared could not inappropriately be described as 'supernatural'". Andrews ordered the journalists to stay on the hill, while he and Delgado, with BBC producer John McNish and a NTV camera crew in tow, made their way down to the field to look at the circles more closely.

THE FIELD GUIDE

Unfortunately for Andrews and Delgado, the indistinct blue things they had ignored on the hill turned out to be board games called Zodiac Spells, placed beneath crossed sticks in the centre of each of the six circles. And with the cameras there and half of Fleet Street watching from the hill there was no chance of ignoring them.

It was against their nature, but Andrews and Delgado would have to admit the circles were a hoax, and they and the crew retired to a nearby pub to straighten their story and put off the inevitable. Two hours later, they returned to the hilltop site carrying the board games and the sticks. Andrews made his announcement to the expectant crowd:

> *As soon as I saw the edges of the first circle, I could tell at once it was an obvious hoax... An inspection on the ground showed very severe damage – bruising, severance, and disturbances consistent with human feet... This affair has improved our credibility, as we were able to detect a hoax within seconds... our equipment can tell within seconds whether a ring is a hoax or not... It even detected the heat of the bodies of the perpetrators!*

But as Andrews spoke the crowd rapidly dwindled, realizing that beyond Andrews' eternally upbeat euphemisms there was very little to see.

The next day, Andrews received a letter which read:

The Beginning

Colin,

the circles on Wednesday were just a hoax,
but we can't help to play jokes.
Inconvenience caused? We're sorry.
Catch us, you'll have to hurry.
Yours, in total control,
the Justified Ancients of Mu Mu - the Jamms.

Try not to worry too hard.
We find it very funny,
While you sit back and rake in the money.

At the bottom of the page was the cryptic message "25 31 Wiltshire" alongside a symbol representing the logo of KLF. The same symbol, a ghetto-blaster superimposed on a pyramid, was found neatly flattened in a Wiltshire wheat field a few days later. This time, however, experts were able to dismiss it as a hoax immediately, a fact confirmed by the farmer who was paid £350 by Drummond *et al.*

THE FIELD GUIDE

The KLF *in post-crop circle retirement.*

REVELATIONS

The 1991 Cornference in Glastonbury was the final weekend of cerealogy's golden years. Michael Green gave a lecture entitled "Breaking the Code of the Agriglyphs", in which he compared the crop pictograms with South American Petroglyphs and rare examples of Atlantean writing. As such, his translation of the Milk Hill Script was something of a *pièce de résistance.*

After playing his slowed-down Dictaphone analysis of the "sound of the circlemakers", Colin Andrews warned that the circles phenomenon rang an ecological alarm call that we would ignore at our peril, even if we shut our ears to his streaming metaphors:

The Beginning

"On the timeline of destiny the clock is ticking and it says five minutes to midnight!"

A curious moment followed when his co-researcher Pat Delgado took to the stage, to Colin's evident dismay, to announce that something important was about to happen. It was imminent! He couldn't quite bring himself to describe what it was but it didn't sound good.

Colin was obviously embarrassed, but managed to calm things down by relaying another message, this one from a Hopi chieftain he had met on his travels. It was no less ambiguous than Pat's, but its poignancy was immediate: "Mother is crying!" He meant Mother Earth. Perhaps that was what Delgado was trying to tell us, but emotion overcame him. It was a curiously unifying moment amidst all the claptrap and suspicion.

The late Richard Andrews (no relation to Colin), a "Gentleman Farmer" from Hampshire, then walked to the front and performed a simple experiment – it is always important to look at a New Science scientifically, he said assuringly in his vicar's voice. The experiment consisted of Andrews dowsing the breadth and intensity of a line of energy he claimed ran down the central aisle, separating the audience. It was barely discernable, he said. What was needed was for the audience to unify, for us all to think alike, as one. After a few minutes of audience meditation, Andrews dowsed it again. Yes, he confirmed, the line was now much wider and stronger, a revelation that many in the audience met with gasps and applause. "There, you see?" said the dowser confidently. "That is what prayer is all about."

At the end of an otherwise unmemorable sermon Richard Andrews advised the audience that, in future, entrance to the circles should be restricted to serious researchers, like himself, rather than just anyone being allowed to visit them, so that they may conduct proper scientific research undisturbed. In an emergent field of study in which no-one could justifiably claim expertise, it was striking how readily people were prepared to accept this kind of hierarchical arrogance, as if happy to contribute to restoring a natural balance of disempowerment. It was all terribly English.

Then came John Michell. He was a hard act to precede, because unlike most of those who came before him he seemed completely at ease bathing publicly in deep esoterica. In contrast to the woolly ambiguities of the previous speakers, Michell was armed with real evidence of almost tangible significance in the form of *pi, phi*, mystical numbers and measurements, which he proceeded to apply to an impressive formation which had appeared that summer in lush green wheat near an ancient Wiltshire hillfort known as Barbury Castle.

An aerial photograph of the pattern flashed onto the screen behind him, followed by a detailed plan drawing. The formation consisted of a circle with two outer rings overlaid

The Beginning

upon a fine-lined equilateral triangle, its sides running between the two rings. From the centre of the pattern came three lines, four feet wide (staunchly anti-metrication, Michell spoke only in Imperial or even older measures). At the apex of each angle sat a ring, each of a different design: the first was a simple ring transected by a line extending from the formation's centre to its own; another was sliced into six curved segments, like spokes on a moving wheel, and another, more of a spiral than a ring, ratcheted inwards incrementally every 45 degrees.

Michell's talk was astounding. Each side of the triangle, he declared, was six times the radius of the corner rings, in keeping with the six segments and six steps of the wheel and ratchet rings. The area of the three rings fit exactly into the area of the largest central ring, demonstrating the ancient principle of Three in One. A similar design, perhaps an inspiration, featured in Stephan Michespacher's 1654 book *Cabala in Alchymia* as an image of the very process of Creation, the three extremities – variously said to represent salt, sulphur and mercury, or water, fire and light, depending on fashion of the time – held in equilibrium until activated by the Creator.

The whole structure contains intrinsic numeric, musical and geometrical harmonies, said Michell: first, "the sum of all the four circular areas in the diagram is 31680 square feet... In traditional cosmology, this was taken to be the measure around the sub-lunary world, and the early Christian scholars calculated the number 3168 as emblematic of Lord Jesus Christ." Michell informed us with a learned authority that few dared question that 316.8 was the number of feet in the circumference of the lintel ring at Stonehenge and was repeated at St Mary's Chapel in Glastonbury, just around the corner. Michell went on: "The number 3168 is superabundant, the Pythagorean term for a number which is exceeded by the sum of its factors. The sum of all the numbers which divide into 3168 is 6660, connecting the number of the Lord Jesus Christ – the Cosmic Christ – with that of the Beast of Revelation." To Michell, the formation was nothing less than "a divine revelation."

It was a fine display of the art of Gematria, based on the principle that every letter of the Greek and Hebrew alphabets has an assigned number. These can be worked into words or phrases, and even theological concepts. In Greek, as Michell rightly said, the letters of "Kurious Iesous Xristos" amount to 3168.

Michell went on. The harmonic 31,680 (six miles in feet) was a sublunar distance related to The New Jerusalem, which he had personally mapped out by dowsing such ancient sites as Stonehenge and Avebury, as well as various crop circles. The figure is derived from a box drawn around the earth, giving 4 x 7920 miles. Moreover, it can be found in a diagram of the moon touching the earth, with a large circle around the earth that passes through the centre of the moon. The circumference of the large circle is 31,680 miles.

If he had not been limited by conventional parameters of time, Michell might

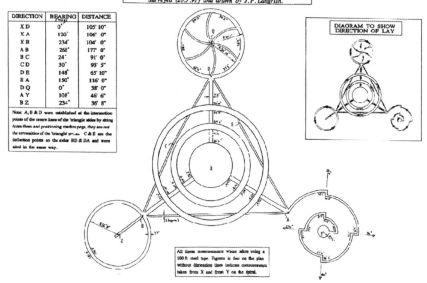

DIRECTION	BEARING	DISTANCE
X D	0°	105' 10"
X A	120°	106' 0"
X B	234°	104' 0"
A B	268°	177' 0"
B C	24°	91' 0"
C D	30°	93' 5"
D E	148°	65' 10"
E A	150°	116' 0"
D Q	0°	38' 0"
A Y	108°	46' 6"
B Z	234°	36' 8"

Note: A, B & D were established at the intersection points of the centre lines of the 'triangle' sides by string down them and positioning marker pegs, they are not the extremities of the 'triangle' proper. C & E are the deflection points on the sides BD & DA and were sited in the same way.

BARBURY CASTLE CROP FORMATION (17:7:91)
SCALE 1:400 ORDNANCE SURVEY GRID REF. SU 152 768 CROP TYPE WHEAT
Surveyed (20.7.91) and drawn by J.F. Langrish.

DIAGRAM TO SHOW DIRECTION OF LAY

All linear measurements where taken using a 100 ft steel tape. Figures in feet on the plan without dimension lines indicate measurements taken from X and from Y on the spiral.

Barbury Castle *diagram by John Langrish.*

have revealed more about the material that can be found in Gematria literature. For example, it is said that even though the earth's orbital path is elliptical, mathematically and symbolically it can be treated as a circle, in which case the distance from the Sun to Earth would be 93 million miles. That's 5892480 inches, give or take a few zeros. Divide this figure by the speed of light, a little under 186,000 miles per second, (again dropping the zeros) and the result will be 3,168. He may also have supposed that Christ was born in the town of Bethlehem, rather than the larger Jerusalem, because Bethlehem sits on the latitude of 31.68°N.

It all sounded uncannily like Umberto Eco's *Foucault's Pendulum*, which was popular in esoteric circles at the time. In chapter 48 (of 120, a mystical number), the protagonists are discussing the work of a one-time Astronomer Royal of Scotland, Charles Piazzi Smyth (1819-1900). For Smyth was also a pyramidologist (or "pyramidiot" as sceptic Martin Gardner famously described him*). Like Michell's and Michael Green's vision of the circles, it was clear to Smyth that mere humans – least of all Egyptians, with their "vile hieratic system" – are incapable of building anything so divine as the Great Pyramid. The proof is easy, consider the numbers…

99

It is worth reproducing Eco's passage. The discussion concerns Piazzi Smyth's classic, *Our Inheritance in the Great Pyramid*, published in 1880 and still in print:

> *I imagine that your author [Smyth] holds that the height of the*
> *pyramid of Cheops is equal to the square root of the sum of the areas*
> *of all its sides. The measurements must be made in feet, the foot being*
> *closer to the Egyptian and Hebrew cubit, and not in meters, for the metre*
> *is an abstract length invented in modern times. The Egyptian cubit comes*
> *to 1.728 feet. If we do not know the precise height, we can use the*

* GARDNER, MARTIN. *Fads and Fallacies in the Name of Science*, (NEW YORK: DOVER PUBLICATIONS, 1957).

The Beginning

pyramidion, which was the small pyramid set atop the Great Pyramid, to form its tip. It was of gold or some other metal that shone in the sun. Take the height of the pyramidion, multiply it by the height of the whole pyramid, multiply the total by ten to the fifth, and we obtain the circumference of the earth. What's more, if you multiply the perimeter of the base by twenty-four to the third divided by two, you get the earth's radius. Further, the area of the base of the pyramid multiplied by ninety-six times ten to the eighth gives us one hundred ninety-six million eight hundred and ten thousand square miles, which is the surface area of the earth. Am I right?

100

It is interesting how Michell's picture of the Barbury Castle formation as measurably, perfectly divine is so far from the measurements of researcher John Langrish, who conducted a careful survey of the site. Michell's findings were more to do with wishful thinking than accurate plotting or surveying. In reality, each side of the triangle was of a different length by as much as ten feet, and each ring was of a different diameter making a mockery of the claim about the 6:1 ratio of the radii to the sides. The smallest radius was 40' 8" to its outer edge, which when multiplied by six comes to 240'. The longest side was the bent one at 184' 5", more than 50 feet short. The bend was due to a minor miscalculation, adjusted "in progress" to steer clear of the ring.

Similarly, the discrepancies undermine Michell's claim that the combined area of the three elements fits into the area of the central outer ring. At 40' 8", 42' and 50' 6" respectively, the total square footage of the rings amounts to approximately 18,595 sq ft, while the area of the outer central ring is approximately 15,418 sq ft. The sum of these, incidentally, amounts to around 34,014, rather more than the claimed 31,680 - but what is a few thousand square feet between humans and deities? Probably quite a lot, to a numerologist.

There can be little doubt that Michell was already familiar with the geometry, albeit an idealised version. And considering the less-than-perfect field measurements, it is possible to imagine a likely scenario behind the pattern's creation. Someone with an intimate appreciation of John Michell's interests, who is also a circlemaker, sets out to make a crop formation that is tailor-made to the Gematriac calculations. The idea may even have indirectly come out of a conversation with Michell. At the time, such "predictions" were commonplace, and there were certainly precedents for this kind of interactivity in UBI's portfolio. In short, the Barbury Castle formation was back-engineered, but not as accurately as Michell would have us believe.

If the central outer ring stayed the size it was, around 70ft, and the elemental rings were each 41 ft in radius, they would have represented the division of the central ring by the Golden Section; 41.6666666666ft to be exact. But this figure squared then multiplied by 3 and added to the area of 70ft (15393.84sq ft) amounts to slightly more than 31680. By adding 12 inches to the radius of the central ring and reverting the radii of the elemental rings back to 41 ft we arrive at 31679.8944, with room in the central ring for the combined area of the three extremities. At just a few inches off 31680, this is impressively close to Michell's claim. If only the circlemaker's loose workmanship hadn't let him down.

Just as Martin Gardner observed of Piazzi Smyth, John Michell's belief in his ideas on the circles was supported by his extraction of a web of seemingly self-consistent numerical correlations, all reliant on the lure of elegant and persuasive writing to hide any factual discrepancies. This is pseudoscience at its very smoothest. The only salient fact that it was necessary to remember about the Barbury Castle formation is that most people would not bother to check the measurements.

THE END OF THE BEGINNING

After the Cornference, George Wingfield invited a few circles insiders back to his house in nearby Shepton Mallet, for early evening drinks. Michael Green was there, basking in the glory of having cracked the Milk Hill scripture, along with Shauna Crockett-Burroughs, editor of a New Age magazine, and an engaging couple, always friendly, called

THE FIELD GUIDE

Researcher *George Wingfield looks perplexed.*

Judy and Peter Young, who ran a company making clothing emblazoned with the latest crop circles designs. As the guests were chatting, George's wife Gloria called her husband to the telephone. It was Pat Delgado, and when George went off she remarked that there was something odd about Pat's voice. It was a mechanical voice, he was talking like a robot.

"He said his name was Zirka, but I recognised him as Pat because he's always phoning", said Gloria in the way she had that left an impression that she found anything George was involved in all rather amusing.

The Beginning

Eventually, Wingfield emerged white-faced. He called Michael Green onto the lawn, out of earshot of his guests. Soon afterwards they left, with Gloria, and the party was over.

Hours later, the now-defunct *Today* newspaper revealed Doug and Dave's activities with the headline "THE MEN WHO CONNED THE WORLD". Their token victim, an established crop circles "expert" ready to agree the genuineness of a test circle, was Pat Delgado. As much as his co-author Colin Andrews tried to neutralise events, Delgado took it badly, and the pair soon went their separate ways. Following the publication of another book a year later, possibly written to satisfy their original book deal, Delgado retired from the scene.

While his book *Conclusive Evidence?* featured a Doug and Dave-inspired pictogram on its cover, in the years that followed Delgado's opinion on their provenance changed dramatically. In a letter written in 1996 to researcher Chris Fowler, in answer to his question of how many circles might be hoaxed, Delgado writes:

> *The complex patterns are not hoaxes, they are genuine man made*
> *artistic flattened crop designs in their own right. The "genuine"*
> *circles are simple single circles and their history probably goes back*
> *thousands of years.*

SEEDLINGS:
THE NEXT GENERATION

Seedlings

Following the *Today* revelations, those who were drawn to the circles phenomenon by the colourful claims of Andrews, Delgado and other experts, and the ensuing media coverage, withdrew just as quickly. For most people, the mystery was fleeting and they moved on. For others, meanwhile, such is their intellectual and emotional investment in a mystery that, once it is exploded, it takes something just as big to fill the void.

An investment in the printed word can be just as hard to reverse. In small worlds, such as science and cerealogy, books and articles can bring a certain status which, when the claims therein become redundant, can be difficult to abandon completely. The same often applies to groups centred around specific beliefs, formed to provide security of numbers against challenges from non-believers. The accommodation of contradictory information need not always be painful, however, for there is a certain caché in digging out a deeper mystery while lesser souls are giving up. After all, as the seer Arthur C Clarke famously observed, what we perceive as magic today could be tomorrow's science.

Colin Andrews had invested more than most. As a direct result of his circles activities he had left his cushy job with the local Council, parted from his wife and family, remarried and set up home in America, where he now earned his living lecturing about crop circles. But at least he could tell himself that the worst had happened *after* he had published a best seller, which is more than could be said for the likes of Michael Green and George Wingfield, and a few others who saw pound signs in the crop circles

Doug & Dave *share a laugh over George Wingfield.*

symbolism. Wingfield took the news of Doug and Dave particularly badly, seeing them as agents of a State cover-up of the truth about crop circles. Adding this idea to a similar explanation for the Blackbird fiasco, identifying other culprits in the process, he regaled anyone who would listen – enough people to justify a tour of the US – with tales of suppression in the name of the Military Industrial Complex, their Intelligence agencies, the Vatican and Opus Dei, until audiences deemed his message too negative and lost interest. While the negativity confirmed that there was something truly phenomenal to the circles, it was best not to dwell too much on it for fear of contributing to it.

107

Perhaps the hardest aspect of the circles to leave behind was their aesthetic magic, and that alone ensured good audiences, regardless of causal agency. But this perspective inevitably leads to the celebration of human artfulness – the diametrically opposite message to the one favoured by worshippers and phenomenalists. Consequently, any evidence of a human hand behind the crop circles was quickly dismissed as "hoaxing", and the messengers vilified as disinformers. Interestingly, for a community in which truth is relative to human experience, and where all manner of djinns and devas play their part – with anecdotal tales of, say, "alien abduction" or "missing time" going mainly unquestioned – the simple story of a human prank that spiralled outward was surprisingly hard to swallow. It went against consensual belief, and was therefore regarded with uncommon scepticism.

As a study in human behaviour it carried echoes of the past. After the sharp rise and fall of fascism during the 1930s and 40s, in the 1950s sociologist Leon Festinger conducted studies comparing contemporary millennarian cults with established religions, such as the American Millerite movement. As with the latter's Great Disappointment of October 22, 1844, he was interested in how communities reacted when prophecy failed and hopes were dashed.

Festinger observed that to varying degrees we strive to preserve a sense of consistency in our beliefs by adapting new, potentially threatening information to suit ourselves, tending to opt for familiarity rather than confront the danger of the new, or the humiliation of being proved wrong. These findings were incorporated into Festinger's later work, *The Theory of Cognitive Dissonance* (1957).

Infiltrating a group of flying saucer enthusiasts, Festinger's team observed firsthand their reaction when a specific prediction – contact with a flying saucer, the group being taken aboard and away to another world – failed to materialise. As with the aftermath of the *Today* story and subsequent "hoaxing" revelations, those with the most to lose appropriated and interpreted information to meet their own and the group's ends. Followers were of course free to either confront any disparities in the information, or accept it as true. For many, and many since, faced with this choice, rather than challenging their existing belief, the disconfirmation only served to confirm and even strengthen it.

Naturally, this level of counterintuitive persistence of belief is most evident in groups, where the status quo is more easily maintained by a common intolerance to contrary information, and any threat to group stability can be effectively separated and rejected. To behave this way alone might seem, to others, mad, but collectively it is more easily excused. The science satirist and philosopher Charles Fort noted a similar process in the way dogmatic scientists react to any challenge to their authority; he referred to the rejected data or ideas as "the Damned". But even purveyors of admirably damnable ideas, once they have achieved some sort of academic credibility, can become just as closed to dissenting opinion.

"Draw a circle around a stone and the stone becomes an object of mystery", wrote the mythographer Joseph Campbell. Charles Fort used a similar illustration…

Seedlings

Just as would one who draws a circle in the sea, including a few
waves, saying that the other waves, with which the included are
continuous, are positively different, and stakes his life upon maintaining
that the admitted and the damned are positively different.

…to show how real and "false" phenomena – as with "genuine" and "fake" and sometimes truth and myth – are continuous and interactive. Consider, for example, the following passage from the CCCS publication *1991 – Scientific Evidence for the Crop Circle Phenomenon,* by Montague Keen:

As the formations had grown in complexity, so the hoax hypothesis had
become more attractive. The more they exhibited patterns inconsistent
with the product of any known or possible natural phenomenon, the
more viewers were forced to choose. And the choice was between the
disturbing – and for some wholly unacceptable – concept of a directing
intelligence, and the more comforting assurance that hoaxers had become
more cunning and skilled, and we could therefore sleep easy and forget
all about it.

It is a good example of how the same argument became politicised, each side using it to suggest that the other was a victim of cognitive dissonance, drowned in a sea of untruth by their reluctance to abandon ship. Interestingly, Monty Keen was one who eventually ceded to the overwhelming evidence of human circlemaking presented to him, only, however, to be vilified himself by the diehards.

Festinger suspected that such intolerance to ambiguity, by groups or individuals, indicated a predisposition for authoritarianism. (And there is no shortage of "bum bailiffs" engaged in paranormal pursuits to support the theory.) It does not always follow that alternative belief systems equate to open-mindedness – take, for example, the 17th century puritans who escaped religious persecution in one country only to practice it in another. As Voltaire wrote a century later, "Those who can make you believe absurdities can make you commit atrocities."

Dave Chorley died in 1996, as have two core members of UBI since their circle-making days in the late '80s to early '90s. Conspiracist circles researcher Paul Vigay has speculated that according to unnamed sources Chorley was looking to "spill the beans" about the "real story" behind the *Today* newspaper revelation – presumably, this was that they were put up to it by the State – but he was assassinated before Vigay was able to interview him.

The power of such a myth is that not only is it impossible to *dis*prove to people who would rather believe it, but it also indirectly, and without any need for evidence, brings into question the honesty of Doug Bower. Thus, it can be said that if their testimony is persuasive, and Doug's material evidence convincing – for example, that he took

Dave Chorley *awaiting orders from his paymasters.*

photographs of the Westbury circles that were harvested before Dr Meaden saw them (*see page 67*), and pre-date Andrews' and Delgado's involvement by a year or more – this is because it was manufactured and backed by the unlimited resources of their paymasters. The fact that Chorley died a natural death makes the tale unlikely, to say the least, but it is typical of the type of appeal to less perceptive reasoning that still holds currency in the crop circles community.

Meanwhile, back in reality, until recently Bower continued making crop circles with new teams that emerged in his wake, who saw him as their symbolic mentor. If the relationship between circlemakers operating "openly" as covert artists and the community of people who believe that their work has otherworldly origins is simple from the artists' perspective – where mingling and gaining feedback from an audience is not unusual – it is unique to the extent that the creators of paranormal phenomena openly participate in the wider social forum that their work has spawned. To demand a seat at the table of people who detest them may not be good etiquette, but it offers an invaluable insight into the role of the scapegoat, and the machinery of projection and denial that makes them such.

And here we reach a fork in the path of recent history, bringing it up-to-date. In the last 15 years, circlemakers have continued in the way of Doug and Dave: working to push the limits of what is perceived to be humanly possible, with each year's efforts extending this perception further, always just out of reach, creating an experiential tension between our world, or our reality, and our innate attraction to the otherworldly.

The other path has been walked, not stomped, by those who have looked to science to validate this perception, while at the same time usurping such traditional convention with new science of their own. In the long tradition of Greek tragedy, a *deus ex machina* descends at the last to rescue the plot...

SCIENCE AND THE CIRCLES

When a man understands he extends his mind and comprehends all
things, but when he does not understand he makes things out of himself
and becomes them by transforming himself into them.
Giambattista Vico (1668-1744)

THE FIELD GUIDE

"You wanna know how it was made?" said the man. He was blonde, bronzed and clearly well-fed, wearing a white shirt and scandals. He was standing in a heart-shaped crop circle and he wanted to talk about it. He spread his arms, as if showing off the view from his penthouse: "It's fantastic, isn't it?"

And it was. The chosen field contained strong, neatly-drilled green wheat, which flattened beautifully, laying down like a soft bouncy carpet. It was mid July, the best time for making the circles that inspire this kind of theatre-in-the-round. This one had been made the previous day, for a "wedding", of sorts – it was more of an art performance piece. But the performance had not ended there...

"It was made by a magnetic bomb in two seconds. *Pow!*", he said, the last word emphasised by fist smacking into palm. "I have evidence!"

Likewise, there is evidence that the patterns are irradiated, magnetised and degravitated, the plants scorched, stretched, swelled and blistered. They are beautifully woven and *oooooze* anomaly. Their shapes, according to one expert, encode, or have encoded within them, obscure mathematical theorems "showing how the floors of laid plants are swirled in mathematical proportions relative to the Golden Mean, the fundamental vortex used by nature to create organisms such as shells, sunflowers, galaxies, even the spatial relationship of the bones in the human hand."*

*HTTP://WWW.LOVELY.CLARA.NET/EDUCATION.HTML

Science

Every human society allots power to a priest class, and in western culture that often means scientists. As with the role of shaman in tribal societies, when ultimate judgement is required on the workings of the physical world (medicine and psychology included) it is scientists we look to as arbiters of truth. Take, for example, the "Sudden Infant Death Syndrome" crisis of 2005, settled in the UK courts, so we thought, on the strength of one individual's expert testimony. The principle of falsifying claims to truth is an accepted safeguard, built-in to the scientific process, as was demonstrated here, where the sole "expert" testimony was successfully challenged and innocent mothers were eventually released from jail. Having learned to look up to the elevated status of the scientist, we are only now beginning to accept that they are as prone to disagreements in their interpretations of data as anyone, and that this lies at the very heart of science philosophy.

While self-correcting mechanisms, principally peer-review and the replication of experimental results, carry their own inherent problems, an agreed approach to science is crucial because it means that the same ground walked by a pioneer can be carefully gone over by others, the finer points better understood and any oversights exposed. Without such a practical, methodical system we would understand much less of the world.

But these problems are particularly relevant to scientists looking at paranormal phenomena. Firstly, a scientist with an otherwise faultless methodological approach may make common assumptions that are likely to go unquestioned by his "peers", who are naturally unfamiliar with the unknown, and probably have little idea of the intricate goings-on within a narrow field of study. In other words, if the methodology appears sound, they may be inclined to take the rest on trust. An example follows where numerous crop circles-related findings were published by an established scientific journal, only for its editors to concede, years later, their glaring pseudoscientific failings. As for replication, so many "paranormal" phenomena are defined by their fleeting nature that it is perhaps *un*scientific to argue that unless it is captured and replicated it can be assumed not to exist. Absence of evidence is not evidence of absence. Consider, as an example, that it took decades for rumours of stones falling from the skies to gain official scientific recognition of meteorites.

To hardened Infallibists, the idea that a scientist will knowingly ignore these norms is deeply shocking. Indeed, in setting any segment of society apart we only set ourselves up for surprise when they inevitably turn out to be just like "us". We are not rationalists, we rationalise, and the world we experience is not an objective reality – it is filtered through theories, knowledge, emotion and associations, and so on. Our natural instinct to make sense of our perceptions – the desire for order – can be so strong that the obvious is easily obscured, with the mundane emerging as mysterious, magnifying the merest conjecture into astounding fact. This process of accommodation is a significant ingredient of many paranormal studies. An example is the way the American astronomer Percival Lowell "saw" canals on Mars. Once he had interpreted the changing colours of the Martian surface as changes in vegetation, it was "only rational" to think that sophisticated life also existed there. It followed that it would require water, hence the canals; *ergo*, an

Science

advanced civilisation built them. Scientists make mistakes, and as they are just as inclined as the rest of us to shape their understanding into line with preconceived views, they can also delude themselves. Furthermore, just as in wider society sometimes a quest can be so crucial that they are even prepared to dissemble the truth and deceive others. This is not a criticism of scientists, merely an acceptance that they are human.

It is argued* that scientific deviance reflects a rapidly changing world as the links between academic science and industry become less easily distinguishable. In the area that concerns us, though, the difference between scientists who strive above all else to maintain high ethical standards and those who are concerned only with pursuing desired "scientific" results may simply come down to preordained belief. As we shall see, the scientific ideal of an unbiased and disinterested approach can be quickly, almost indiscernibly, skewed by one convenient assumption, or by ignoring an inconvenient fact. We should remember, also, that myths (out-of-date knowledge) can come about by the same sorts of approach that lead to scientific knowledge – indeed, it is possible that any myth *was* once the best knowledge available.

If the line drawn between scientists and non-scientists appears neatly defined, pseudoscience smudges it. As, occasionally, does art. This may be disruptive and upsetting to those who prefer to see knowledge as an orderly progression, but in the wider scheme of things it may not be a bad thing, because order is based on existing experience whereas to

*Scientific Deception: An Update LESLIE GRAYSON, THE BRITISH LIBRARY 1997

engage with the new requires risk.

By its status, Science, with a capital "S", like the Catholic Church, invites a contradictory relationship with its novices. On one hand, as a systematic means of study it is something solid and respectable to be aligned with, and on the other it is an exclusive gateway that, without the right requirements for entry, it is necessary for those who feel excluded to break into by other means – usually by mimicry and impersonation. However, the type of scientific "impostor" involved in crop circles research (or any of the, let's say, "new sciences") is not bogus in the traditional sense. They are not usually the kind who pretend to be doctors or hold academic posts, but in exercising their right to investigate a mystery they give off subtler cues of their would-be association with the establishment: word and protocol-perfect scientific papers; impressive equations and graphs, "black box" tools with lights, dials and a fancy title etc. Or sometimes the device might be as simple and effectual as a clean white coat.

Science

AN ELIXIR OF FRAUD

One of the earliest laboratory analyses of a crop circle was conducted in 1990 by Signalysis Ltd, a pharmaceutical facility operated from the Stroud, Gloucestershire, home of Kenneth and Rosemary Spelman. Their "spagyrik therapy" was sold as both diagnosis and treatment in one, and for all manner of life-threatening ailments. First, they advised a diagnosis *before* symptoms were apparent. Once illness was ascertained, the cure entailed the distillation and evaporation of mixed extracts of blood and urine from the patient. The resultant ash was then analysed under a microscope, mixed with herbs, diluted with water and returned for oral administration to the patient. It was said that Mrs Spelman had a peculiar skill when it came to interpreting microscopic patterns in samples, and encouraged by circles researchers she turned this talent to analysing essence of wheat. From this she produced vials of "crop circle remedy", available at £17 with an optional silver chain.

First promoted by Andrews and Delgado in their best-selling *Circular Evidence,* the banner for spagyrik analysis was picked up by another circles commentator, Freddy Silva, who assures his readers that the procedure is "approved in the German Government's *Pharmacopoeia for Homeopathy* for spagyric preparations – a process normally used in the diagnosis of human blood samples". The Spelman's results of crop circle analysis, he tells us, "revealed how the irregular pattern in control samples had taken on a strict structuring pattern inside crop circles – energy of some type had changed the plants' crystalline structure." (quoted from *www.cropcirclesecrets.org*)

THE FIELD GUIDE

Silva does not mention the problems the Spelmans faced as their work drew scrutiny from medical professionals, journalists, and then the Royal Pharmaceutical Society (RPS). First there was a TV documentary on alternative medicine featuring treatment of the reporter, an AIDS sufferer – his "cure" contained bacteria that could have killed him. Persistent complaints led to a hearing in which the RPS disciplined the Spelmans, warning other pharmacists that they would be struck off if they associated themselves in any way with spagyrik therapy. As the Spelmans were not registered pharmacists they were found guilty of misconduct under Section 80(1)(b) of the Medicines Act. Their prime witness, a German doctor, was described by the committee as "apparently willing to make any claim that he thought he could get away with by obfuscation"*.

A LITMUS TEST OF GENUINENESS

Microscopic differences were one thing, but, as one early researcher observed, it is hard to carry an electron microscope into a wheat field – what was required were changes to affected and unaffected plants that anyone could detect immediately. A litmus test of "genuineness".

But first it was necessary to define genuineness. The assumption that it is more than just an abstract concept created a rush to find differences to support it. This hunt for anomalies led, in 1991, to an observation by Kay Larsen, a retired biology teacher from

*BRITISH MEDICAL JOURNAL 13TH SEPTEMBER 1997

Science

Cornwall, that not only were the growth nodes on young barley stems from a flattened circle bent and enlarged, but some of them had "exploded". He thought this was a condition that could only have been caused by an "unknown, unidirectional force". Because circles were known to appear quickly, Larsen proposed that this was by way of a short burst of intense heat. He later went on to achieve the bending effect in a microwave oven, which softened the plants enough to manipulate them by hand – it was replication of sorts.

Understandably at this time, few circles researchers had much experience of studying crops and how they grow, let alone how they react to being flattened. Not that this was entirely overlooked. In 1990, at the First International Conference on the Circles Effect, organised by Dr Terence Meaden and held under the dreaming spires of Oxford University, agronomist John Graham submitted a paper titled *The Nature of Damage to Plants in Corn Circles*. Based on observations of "lodged" or wind-damaged crops, it described "geotropic cell elongation" as a part of a plant's natural recovery response. Dr Graham went into more detail in further correspondence to researcher Paul Fuller:

> *Cells in the nodes on the side closest to the ground elongate and*
> *stretch. Tiny pits in those cell walls seem to stretch and alter shape*
> *automatically, particularly in the uppermost nodal regions (where*
> *plant tissue is younger, less thick and more pliable). In the unaffected*
> */unlodged crop cell stretching is less common and more uniform, hence*
> *the difference between samples and controls described by Levengood.*

THE FIELD GUIDE

WC (William) Levengood, that is, a career biologist with a broad range of scientific experience. In semi-retirement he ran a small laboratory out of his house in Michigan, USA. Of all the lasting legacies of Andrews' and Delgado's book *Circular Evidence* perhaps most significant is that it elicited a letter, in 1991, from Levengood to Delgado asking for samples of genuine crop circles to be sent to him for study. The scientist presumably took it on trust that Delgado, a fellow scientist, was able to determine genuine from non-genuine, after all, from his book he sounded like he knew what he was talking about:

> *The greatest of all physicists, Albert Einstein, proved that photons exist, but they do not exist in time. In other words, they do not recognise time. He also stated that everything in existence is based upon the photon. The photon has an infinite lifetime, and can take any form it wishes as mass and anti-mass. With the anti-proton, or photon, which has no mass and no charge, an infinite lifetime is established as the vital bridge between the state of being (now) and the state of "not being" in the physical world. This would seem to support the theory that the circles are created by an unknown force field manipulated by an unknown intelligence. – Pat Delgado, in* Circular Evidence

On receipt of the bag of dried samples that had been collected by Delgado from a circle the previous summer, along with "control" samples of plants from outside the circle,

Science

Levengood set out to identify any differences. Any changes, he assumed, could then be put down to the circlemaking force. He immediately noticed that the seeds were absent from the "genuine" sample. He also identified polyembrony, a rare genetic aberration in which more than one embryo develops in a single glume (the dried leaf shell that grows part way up the stem). Moreover, just as Larsen had surmised, from the bent nodes and the occasional "expulsion cavities" they displayed, Levengood confirmed that the force emitted ionising radiation, possibly, he suggested, by way of some kind of "plasma cloud". Or perhaps a whirlwind? It was all sounding strangely familiar.

Apart from his starting by presuming "genuineness", the second most striking thing about Levengood's early research is that it tended to confirm existing findings, as if the lay-researchers desperately looking to him for answers were being fed a diet of science they already knew. With Larsen withdrawn again into retirement, Dr Meaden had by this time accepted the evidence that some of his ideas were based on man-made circles (evidence Levengood simply ignored), and toned them down accordingly – as Professor Roy commented, the Plasma Vortex now had much less to do than it was invented to undertake. But more than this, not only had Levengood adopted theories abandoned by their parents but he had raised them as his own. Elongated, bent and exploded nodes due to exposure to flash radiation from a "plasma vortex" is an idea now synonymous with Levengood. By design or not, he had succeeded in giving some ill-founded research the stamp of scientific approval.

THE FIELD GUIDE

Meanwhile, to confuse things further, for WC Levengood read BLT Research Team Inc – the letters standing for Levengood, Burke and Talbott. John Burke was a businessman with, as he describes "a university background in physics", while Nancy Talbott claimed a similar research backround but had more recently worked as a country music promoter. After Levengood's early success in analysing the circles, the trio teamed up, aided by funding from Laurence Rockefeller, a philanthropist well-known for his interest in UFOs, and they went on to write several peer-reviewed papers and lab reports. They also diversified into other areas of ufological interest, such as alien abductions and cattle mutilations. Unsurprisingly, these studies tended to confirm the phenomena under examination. In one case reported in *Western Spirit* magazine, a woman approached the team for help in determining the true nature of her night time abduction experiences. Levengood prepared a numbered series of gelatin capsules filled with wheat seeds. The woman was instructed to place one of the gel caps in her hair curlers each night before she went to bed. Levengood later collected the capsules and set about sprouting the seeds. All the samples sprouted normally except for one, which was "dead, totally fried." Sure enough, the sample coincided with the night she felt she had been abducted. "It was like somebody put a microwave to her head," said Talbott. Levengood also found microscopic "pseudo crystals" in dust at the site of an another alleged alien abduction, "that have not been found in dust where abductions are not known to occur."*

* HTTP://WWW.ABDUCT.COM/RESEARCH/R9.HTM

SHAM SCIENCE

A complete list of Levengood's or BLT's scientific claims about crop circles over the past 15 years would be much too long to feature here; suffice to say that any challenge to their observations has been duly absorbed. For example, rather than falsifying their claims, the fact that "anomalies" displayed in crop circles are to be found in weather-damaged or "lodged" crop confirmed to BLT that lodging was itself a random, non-geometric manifestation of the same exotic phenomenon.

BLT Research Team Inc is now run exclusively by Nancy Talbott, who has put her experience in the entertainment industry to good use. Judging from the BLT website she keeps up a busy schedule lecturing at UFO conferences across America and Europe on such topics as: *Common Threads Among Various "Anomalous" Phenomena – Are They Really So Separate?; The Scientific Evidence that Crop Circles are NOT Man-Made, followed by Personal & Eyewitness Accounts which Suggest a Consciousness Behind the Phenomenon* and *The Boy From Holland: Consciousness & the Crop Circles.*

In the latter case, Talbott has taken on the story of Robbert van den Broeke as something of a *cause célèbre*. Van den Broeke is a medium, and like Rita Goold and other mediums he attracts all manner of phenomena: voices from the afterlife, balls of light, alien entities (which he has photographed in the living room at his family home) to crop circles appearing in a field at the end of his parent's garden, preceded, he says, by a cricket-like trilling noise. But evidence has recently surfaced that casts these stories into doubt. The Dutch newspaper *De Telegraaf,* for instance, reported in 2003 that the parents of "a paranormally-gifted child", thought to be Robbert, were caught "vandalising" a field by the farmer, who intended to prosecute. The boy was also caught out on a Dutch TV show when information he passed on from the spirit world to a grieving widow was shown to have emanated – word perfect, even down to a spelling error – from the Google web search engine. Given Talbot's association with an obvious hoaxer it is perhaps unsurprising that few besides committed believers heed her pleas for BLT's science to be taken seriously.

Science

Meanwhile, John Burke has gone on to exploit a patent begat from crop circles research, JA Burke and WC Levengood's *Method and Apparatus for Enhancing Growth Characteristics of Seeds Using Ion-Electron Avalanches* – USA Patent No 5,740,627 (1998) – and now heads a company selling licences for its use, a potentially huge market if it works, and, one would suppose, even if it doesn't. Citing eight years of lab testing (presumably based on Levengood's crop circle research), and six years of field tests, the device, licensed under "MIR or Molecular Impulse Response/Stress Guard™" is, claims the company…

> *…ideally suited for mass production. Large amounts of seed pass*
> *between two electrodes that are calibrated to produce an electrical*
> *impulse specifically targeted for that type of seed. This "electron shower"*
> *initiates a cellular response within the seed that ultimately increases*
> *its growth rate, uniformity and yield while improving its tolerance to*
> *external environmental factors such as drought, flood and temperature*
> *extremes.* – Proseed Technologies, Inc.

Incidentally, in crediting the discovery of the process ("by chance"), Levengood is described as "Dr". In 2001, ufologist Kevin Randle questioned Levengood's academic credentials: the scientist claimed his "PhD equivalent" came from the US National Academy of Sciences, who confirmed to Randle that they make no such awards.

John Burke has also written a book to accompany the product. In *Seeds of*

THE FIELD GUIDE

Knowledge, Stone of Plenty: Understanding the lost technology of the ancient megalith-builders, as the title suggests, Burke reasons that the pyramids of ancient Egypt and South America, the mounds in North America and megalithic sites such as Stonehenge were built, he writes, "for the very practical use of amplifying naturally occurring electro-magnetic fields in the earth in order to increase crop yields – a technology that only recently has been replicated by modern science."

CAPTURING THE IMAGINATION

Its existence "outside" the known natural world makes "the supernatural" notoriously difficult to capture. Using a range of tools, many have claimed an ability to measure elusive phenomena, but to try this is to inevitably become entangled in what is known as the Experimenter's Regress. This occurs because the only way to capture something, and thus prove it exists, is through consensual agreement of what constitutes a proper result, and the only way to achieve this is by performing a valid experiment, and the only way to know it is a valid experiment is by a proper result... and so the cycle continues until it is somehow broken. It is no good waving a wand and just wishing a thing into existence; in order to prove it exists you have to (borrowing Dr Johnson's analogy) kick it, and it has to be *seen* to kick back.

This probably applies to diviners more than most, partly because of the perceived crossover from the dowsing of tangible objects, where empirical evidence

THE CIRCULAR

VOLUME 5:2   Issue 18   Autumn 1994   £2.50

Figure in a Landscape: Vortex Formation at Oliver's Castle, Devizes   *photo: Michael Hesemann*

IN THIS ISSUE

New shapes, new crops, new sites!
Selected reports from Branches and an Illustrated Tour of trends in 1994 designs
Consciousness and quantum changes - the role of our awarenesss explored by *Palden Jenkins*, and *Jazz Rasool*
and - **Polarities of perception** reconciled by *Jim Lyons* and *Stanley Messenger*
Strict measures applied by *Roy Dutton* and Paul *Vigay* to debunkers' claims
Excuse me - your assumption is showing - *Andy Thomas* warns
Milk Hill Yields its secrets - maybe - to *Patricia Villiers-Stuart* and *Pat Selfe*
Drawing the invisible - *Arthur Hamlin* offers his insights into circlemakers and circlemaking
And throughout - **Photographs** and **Phenomenal happenings**
just a few of the weird, wacky and truly wonder - ful experiences reported by croppies

The Journal of the Centre for Crop Circle Studies

is always available and judgement is by results for all to see, and the dowsing of intangibles, where we only have the dowser's word for a "hit", and as sure as they are of their readings and measurements, there are just as many people who are not. But, while full consensus is a distant dream, the vast majority of us are nonetheless impressed by the use of instrumentation. In the right hands, scientific hardware is widely assumed to provide a non-interventionist objectivity over human fallibility, thus eliminating bias. In fact, just like any other element of our material culture it acts as an extension and enhancement of ourselves, magnifying subjectivity. Photography is a good example, as is dowsing (in the wrong hands). Consider Pat Delgado's famous epiphany, reported in his 1992 book *Crop Circles: The Latest Evidence*. Here, the abandonment of the measuring tools leads to complete subjective liberation:

> *I soon realised rods were a hindrance to progress in understanding more about the energies surrounding us. During a session dowsing a tumulus, I became aware I was detecting only a tiny fraction of what was there to be discovered. I abandoned the rods and started to use my bare hands. Immediately a whole new world of information opened up. It was the beginning of my really understanding energies and the intelligence that controls them.*

Opposite: *a cover of the* Circular, *journal of the CCCS, demonstrating some of the scientific ideas popular amongst croppies at the time.*

Science

TAKE TWO HEADS

In the early days of Levengood's research, one of his most vocal supporters was Montague Keen, the Science Advisor to the CCCS. Keen, a one-time agricultural journalist who had a farm himself, had sufficient understanding of the biology of cereals to communicate with Levengood on his level, and even, it transpired, beyond it. Despite his initial enthusiasm, however, after visiting the Michigan laboratory where much of Levengood's scientific procedures were taking place, Keen began to have serious doubts and expressed them in public.

At the instant Monty Keen faulted Levengood's methodology, his role as Science Advisor to the CCCS became untenable. While he was looking for a realistic basis of research into mysterious phenomena, the CCCS were only interested in validating it. In 1995, the dispute tumbled into the welcoming arms of the *Journal of Scientific Exploration* (JSE), where John Burke, on behalf of BLT, mockingly (and unfairly) equated Keen with the mindset of the new Science Advisor to the CCCS, none other than its Chairman, Michael Green. It was an example of just how far, in the absence of Keen's sensible advice, research into crop circles had regressed.

> *Take two cereal heads from the centre of the circle and another two well outside (100 metres) within the same field. Lay them on the bonnet of your car and think "AURA" and dowse them. If there is a difference between the two heads we are dealing with a genuine phenomenon.*

THE FIELD GUIDE

CCCS Procedures for the 1995 Season, Chairman Michael Green
– quoted in *JSE* Vol 9, No 4 letter from Dr Wm Levengood (sic),
John Burke & Nancy Talbot.

Over ten years later, in 2005, Keen's dispute over BLT's and Green's ill-conceived choice of controls was finally put to bed with other pseudoscientific misconceptions – notably, the causal association of "balls of light" and crop circles – by an article in the same journal:

> *...the claims put forward (by Levengood et al) are not supported at all by the available evidence, which on the other hand demonstrates nothing but a mere difference in the stem elongation between the flattened plants lying inside the circles and those standing outside them, as one should expect when whatever kind of mechanical force flattens the plants.*

Balls of Light: The Questionable Science of Crop Circles
Grassi, Cocheo & Russo - *JSE*, Vol. 19, No. 2, 2005.

At this, researchers' pleas for the "science" of crop circles, as promoted by BLT and their kin, to be taken seriously outside the circles community were doomed, which is unfortunate, because it would be a shame if real scientists were to ignore the field completely.

Science

UNEXPLAINED RESEARCH

Lucy Pringle *(opposite)*, ex-CCCS Vice-President and founder of the Unexplained Research Society of Petersfield, Hampshire, represents a feminine, more intuitive approach to crop circles research. It could be argued that Doug and Dave's relationship, with its contrasting styles of piano-string perfectionism and artistic, *laissez faire* spontaneity reflected not only the different approaches to making circles but also to appreciating them – should we treat the patterns as empirical evidence defined by analysis or simply lay back on the soft warm carpet of brushed wheat and absorb the experience without a care for its origins? As one who was cured of a recurring shoulder injury while standing in a crop circle, Pringle was naturally hopeful that the drastic cuts to the local Wiltshire health budget in the mid-1990s were only the start of a positive shift in priorities toward healing, and that her own research would lead the way. Living in the heart of circles country, Pringle was able to amass a wealth of anecdotal and circumstantial evidence that visitors to the formations were indeed experiencing mysterious, spontaneous healings of long-standing ailments and conditions. There was only one way to make sense of these enigmatic cases, and that was to apply the methods of science.

Pringle buried small bottles of water at circles sites, leaving them there for a few days and then measuring the resultant energy resonance by "counting pendulum oscillations" (ie dowsing). These she checked by carefully monitoring "delta activity" (ie intuition). And then she measured the nitrate/nitrogen levels in the soil. True to Pringle's commitment

to "unexplained research", she did not explain why – perhaps to eliminate any variables caused by artificial nutrients? – but on the strength of this research she felt able to assure *Daily Mail* readers that she has a verifiable scientific method for determining "genuine" crop circles from man-made kitsch. And this, alas, is about where things stand today. While only a fool would favour vague, apocryphal, low-grade evidence over practical demonstration, here truth is relative and answers are invariably obscured, as if the spell will be broken by discovery.

GENUINE UNKNOWNS

135

The willingness, personified by Pringle, to imbue the inanimate with "spirit" and then demonstrate an ability to read it has become something of a New Age cliché. While little conflict exists between science and traditional religious faith – by definition, faith exists outside of certainty and carries no aspirations of proof – purveyors of evidence of the "hard" materiality of the supernatural are another matter, for theirs is a culture lost in the uncharted territory of validation. Meanwhile, the limitations of practical physics, malleable as they are, place honest theoretical physicists at something of a disadvantage, for

Science

they operate by the logic of research and discovery – essentially, this starts at *not* knowing – whereas the logic of knowledge needs no discovery because it knows already. While any questioning of faith leaves an uncomfortable taste, a challenge to certainty is far harder to swallow.

What resonates even as strongly as Pringle's pendulum oscillations is the post-rationalist echo of science. The scientific-sounding language and mimicry of convention may show a desire to emulate orthodox scientists, but this new-skin-for-old-ceremonies disguises a deeper truth: honest, systematic scrutiny carries a risk that by physically nailing "mysterious" phenomena their mystique will die. This is what worried Doug Bower when his efforts were explained away as less than otherworldly, and by a scientist no less! How could a scientist get things so wrong? It is even more threatening to those who approach the circles religiously, seeing them as a medium of transcendence to higher realms and higher truth. Observes the historian Felipe Fernández-Armesto:

> *Such truth usually comes with strings attached to human manipulators,*
> *disseminated by dubious experts and interpreted by self-conferred figures*
> *of authority. This is, of course, entirely dependent upon the willingness*
> *of others to accept that authority.*

To keep this truth alive, answers must always be just out of reach and continually reinvented to maintain the distance.

THE FIELD GUIDE

Language is usually assumed to be a guarantee of clarity, but so often in this environment it serves as a useful means of *mis*interpretation. (It was Giambattista Vico, incidentally, who recommended the study of language, ritual and myth as a means of understanding any society, since it is we who fashion them in our own image.) Take the word "genuine", for example. It usually implies a single, identifiable origin, of established provenance, but in croppy culture it means the opposite: "of unknown provenance", or non-man-made. The possibility that man-made circles spawned the very aesthetic – symbolic design, precise edges, a smoothly flowing and layered floor, etc – that *defines* "genuineness" in most people's eyes is conveniently ignored in favour of the abstract unfathomable.

To test this properly is as simple as discreetly making a circle, or a series of circles, and observing how this generates the same effects and claims as the so-called genuine circles. In the absence of better evidence, what we understand today as the "genuine" *is* man-made. Even the leading researcher of his day, Pat Delgado, went on to admit this: "However the circles and patterns are created" he wrote to a researcher in 1996, "some people will always have anomalous experiences in them." The irony is that if Lucy Pringle or one of her students were to drop the "scientific" pretence and actually try to find out any positive benefits to this kind of spiritual phenomenon it might stand a real chance of dislodging the status quo and lead to new paradigms.

138

ART AND PHILOSOPHY

"If you label me, you negate me" Søren Kierkegaard

THE FIELD GUIDE

If the key to the mystery business is in avoiding answers, to the circlemaker Kierkegaard's axiom holds true. Here, in a nutshell, is why circlemakers do not signpost their work as "art", as some have suggested to "clear the waters" and separate the genuine. It also reflects the curious symbiotic relationship between circlemakers and the "researchers" who turn a blind eye to their activities.

This also extends to news media. Every June, as wheat fields mature to their potential as artists' canvasses and the patterns begin to appear, unenlightened hacks take the prettiest ones to date and shroud them in mystery, and there is no shortage of researchers with a vested interest in helping them. Then, as the season comes to a close, the artists responsible are ritually unmasked and the "mystery" revealed, only for the whole charade to begin again the following spring. Over 15 years, this has turned into something of an annual tradition, much like the corn dolly, fashioned to ensure the circles' renewal in the public imagination.

Ultimately, of course, beyond the machinations of the media the circles phenomenon is artist-led, as each year we, the circlemakers, try to outdo ourselves in manifesting the unbelievable and extending perceptions of what is humanly possible. Like all artists, however, even anonymous ones, circlemakers do what we do for others to experience, and feed off the response. In truth, the crop circles would amount to little of artistic merit without audience participation.

Art and Philosophy

When, in 1991, the art critic John McEwen wrote "Who, or whatever makes (the circles) is an artist of genius", he was unaware of Doug Bower's (or even Billy Meier's) inspired act of laying down simple circles to suggest physical contact with alien life. Would he have said the same if he knew? It seems clear that this act revealed a latent, mystical kinship with leucippotomy, the art of cutting chalk horses, practised since the Early Iron Age. Indeed, of all the white horses that decorate the English landscape, the older they are the more they carry a simplicity of form that now seems lost to us – the same genius of restraint that was once also seen in the early modern era of crop circles, when only Doug and Dave were making them.

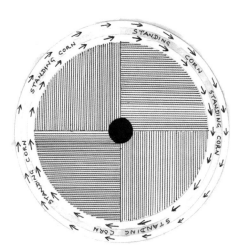

Doug's diagram *for the "swastika" crop circle.*

THE FIELD GUIDE

But McEwen was writing slightly later, and of the "pictograms". Not to take anything away from their makers, perhaps the real genius lies in how these relatively simple designs were accommodated, by the audience, within an established mystical framework of alchemy, rune languages and hieroglyphs, sacred geometry and ancient mandalas, as well as the fractal geometry of chaos theory. And then, in turn, how we integrated it all into late-20th century cultural iconography, as part of an evolving visual language.

Doug's *pictogram doodles.*

It is a collective genius. This would explain why Colin Andrews' Hopi friends "recognised" the symbols as their own, and why similar shapes occur in ancient rock paintings from California to Africa, from Erik Beckjord's obscure Korean/ Tifinag language to Michael Green's Atlantean, and even on the inside of our own eyelids in the form of phosphenes, entoptic visual sensations produced through migraines or chemistry. (It has been argued that non-figurative art of the Upper Paleolithic depicts actual visions of phosphenes and neurological "form constants", perhaps enhanced by hallucinogenic drugs.)

ART OF THE GODS

We fashion gods in many forms, both visible and invisible, all demonstrating an ability to interact with us through symbolism. The primary characteristic of symbolic art is that it can be viewed independently on various levels; we can read it from the multiple perspectives of the artist who makes it, the producer who embellishes and empowers it, the users and audiences who interact with it, and the "shamans" who guard the power stored within. What anthropologist Preston Blier wrote of West African vodun sculpture can also be said of the circles:

> *The most salient features of these artworks are the powerful human emotions they evoke, their potency is a manifestation of their psychological power to disorientate, disturb and grip the imagination; force, fear, fury, shock, disorder and deception play critical roles in their reception and use.*

Given the relationship between art and perception, it is not surprising that an emotional response to perceived phenomena can trigger paranormal experiences. In theatrical terms, the material object itself – in this case, the crop circles – serves as a "MacGuffin", a term coined by the film director Alfred Hitchcock to describe a plot device that is generally accepted by all the central characters and serves as motivation, representing the promise of something bigger. Out of this emerge the rumours and innuendo that drives so much of paranormal research. As Hitchcock describes it:

> *A "MacGuffin" is the name by which we call this sort of action: stealing papers, stealing a document, stealing a secret. The thing is not important in itself, and logicians go wrong in searching for a truth in the MacGuffin. In my work I've always thought that while the papers, the documents or the secret of the construction of a fortress must be important for the characters of the movie, they have to be of no interest to me, to the story-teller.*

Another circlemaker, Jim Schnabel, defined the general principle: "If there can be artifice on the way into the mind, there can be artifice on the way out."

Another example of how we accommodate artifice into suggestion occurred in Mexico City during the total solar eclipse of 1991, when a wave of UFOs were predicted by the host of a popular TV magazine show, who invited viewers to send in their videos of any unusual objects they saw in the sky. Sure enough, hundreds of people sent in videos showing luminous points of light, silently "hovering" as the skies darkened.

Art and Philosophy

Padre Manuel Ferrare sent in a video and was immediately interviewed about it. "I came out to take a shot of a pine tree against the light" said the priest, clearly enjoying his 15 minutes of fame, "I saw a light appear over the mountain. It was not an ordinary light, it was blue and very intense. I have never been afraid of something like this – on the contrary, what I have been able to observe has been wonderful." While his vision made for exciting television, it was possible to tell from the position of the sun that the lights corresponded with the astronomical placement of the planets Venus and Mars and the star Regulus, brightening as daylight dimmed.

We may convince ourselves that experiences such as these, "seen with our own eyes", are entirely objective but the truth is often lost to interpretation, and then it can be sucked along a continuum ranging from optical illusion to pious myopia through varying degrees of self-deception to the active deception of others. As the Catholic art philosopher Jacques Maritain observed, visionaries turn away from nature in favour of an interest in themselves, in their own subjectivity. "Seeking after themselves", he writes, "they are carried along beyond the natural appearance of things in a desperate search of deeper reality". This awakening of creative subjectivity is a role played mutually by artist and mystic – as Maritain describes it, "the classic visionary's conquest of consciousness, subsequently occupied by the mind of the many." The same spirit may have intoxicated Arthur Shuttlewood, for his books provide an interesting insight into the reflective, Rorschachean nature of perceived supernatural phenomena.

THE FIELD GUIDE

Such phenomena *invite* projection, just as the German Romantic poet and spiritualist Justinus Kerner used similar ambiguous devices to "see" ghosts. Likewise it is claimed, by the aesthetician Morse Peckham for example, that we create scenarios intended to provoke inquiry and challenge pre-conceived ideas in order to satisfy a physiological need for something more stimulating than the order-directed environment that society tends to manufacture. Indeed, could all artistic activity fulfil an evolutionary function driving the progress of ideas and knowledge? What if art and the supernatural go so naturally together in this mutual exchange of interpretative interplay because they are bound by the greater good of our collective interaction with the Unknown?

Such phenomena may also reveal themselves as a reminder of something that exists in what Carl Jung called our collective unconscious. A first sighting of a crop circle can often set off vague "memories" of having seen them before, and this might explain some of the more recent historical accounts. That these memories may be false makes them no less evocative, and perhaps all the more alluring.

Bill Ellis, an Associate Professor at Penn State University specialising in semiotics and folklore, uses a term coined by Umberto Eco to define this interactivity: ostension. According to Ellis, ostension is present whenever someone creates a stir by manufacturing evidence for legendary events. Such cases test the boundaries of "life" and "legend" by staging actions that the players represent as real and that the audience overtly accepts as such. Yet, these performances are not always fiction; they may inspire real-life actions with lasting results.

Ostension can be broken down into three sub-categories: pseudo-ostension, proto-ostension and quasi-ostension. The first involves a hoax in which the perpetrator enacts a legend. For example, teenagers killing animals and creating occult symbols as fabricated evidence of satanic cult rituals. It happens. Proto-ostension is where an individual draws from a legend and claims it to be their own experience, transforming a legend into an apparently verifiable first-person account. We need look no further than Rita Goold for evidence of this. Quasi-ostension is where naturally occurring events are misinterpreted as first-hand experience of an existing legend. When aerial light phenomena are observed and automatically associated with the creation of a crop circle, for instance, as with David Kingston's ball of light sighting at Warminster (if indeed this story is true; if not, it would qualify as proto-ostension).

LORDS OF ILLUSION

Like all illusion, the circles should be seen as something other than an intellectual device. Knowledge of how illusions work does not stop us being fooled by them, and our reaction to mystery is fairly consistent – suspending disbelief and entertaining the unknown and indefinable is a magical, creative activity, which works best when we *are* really mystified.

THE FIELD GUIDE

Just as an artist will try to forget the work of other artists in trying to create original work, the mystic distances himself from existing knowledge – all the easier if he's never known it. This type of ignorant enquiry is the very basis of discovery, and is in its purest form grounded in both art and science.

Aesthetics, religion and psychology are all subtly intertwined. In the psychology of mysticism there is a confusion between states of "me" and "not me". Morse Peckham described this mental separation from one's immediate environment as "psychic insulation", a mild trance state. "The creative person" he writes, "is able to see similarities and relationships that are new and unique. But first they must be able to see dissimilarities, and the absence of relationships where traditionally they are found. He sees the emperor has no clothes. He sees absurdities in conventional wisdom." Where the scientist is conditioned to recognise existing relationships, the seer seeks new ones. He enters into a kind of *folie à deux* with the object, making connections that are either invisible or overlooked by others.

Festinger, Peckham, Kuhn, and a broad range of punditry on the evolution of knowledge have all stressed the need for a tension to exist between observation and experience. As in any self-modifying system, "crazy", ill-founded ideas compete with consensual knowledge – and some survive, despite the kicking and screaming of sceptics. This mutation is the raw material of change.

Art and Philosophy

The recognition of false phenomena invites such crucial questions as "What if it were real?" or "What is it about us that makes placebos so effective?" and even "Is there a state that exists *between* the physical and 'all in the mind?'" These kinds of questions encourage the discontinuous, paradigmatical leaps of scientific advance – often achieved, noted the philosopher Paul Feyerabend, by irrational, counter-inductive and "unscientific" methods.

Paradoxically, just as we are beginning to realise the value of play in human development, the wider opportunities for it are diminishing. Rather than seeing value in error, we emphasise its correction, and to venture beyond accepted boundaries is to risk being labelled a fool. But in order to develop we need the constant stimulus of new ideas, even if this means we have to conjure them out of nothing. The artist often fulfils this function, as do potty cloud-gazers and other "cranks".

As with circlemakers and circles "believers", there is an indivisible, insoluble bond between reality and fiction, artists and audience, creator and experiencer, binding those who believe mystery should be adored and those who would play with it. An understanding of these relationships is crucial to discovering the nature of true and false phenomena, especially when they are indistinguishable at their merging points. Circlemaking follows in an abundant tradition of artists who have worked this fusion and specialised in actively stimulating visionary experience. The sculptor James Turrell, for example, whose 1996 exhibition at London's Institute of Contemporary Art was designed to "induce extraordinary visions and sensations, evoking the UFO as both sensory experience and metaphor".

Another is Bill Witherspoon, who in 1990 inscribed a vast traditional mandala, the Sri Yantra, 400 metres across, on the surface of a dry lake bed in the high desert of south-west Oregon. Its 13 miles of lines were ploughed with a garden cultivator, and covered an area of over 40 acres. Witherspoon believes that the power of the shape alone effected changes in the immediate environment and the local wildlife. The soil within it changed from alkaline silt to fertile, while Witherspoon observed that birds and animals were attracted to the vicinity and displayed relaxed and unthreatened behaviour toward

159

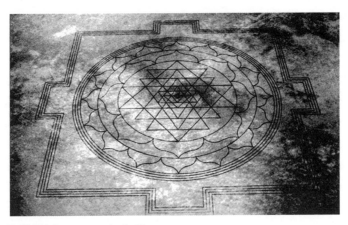

Bill Witherspoon's *Sri Yantra, 1990.*

others. Accordingly, local ranchers noticed an increase in the valley's rainfall, and several plants and three animal species appeared there for the first time. Witherspoon speculates that there is something intrinsic to geometric structures that can initiate change, relating his findings to traditional concepts of spiritual "consciousness" and awareness… "Could an artwork encourage some specific influence of nature to be amplified in the environment?", he asks.

When the pattern was discovered later it attracted flak from environmentalists, who were unimpressed by the theory behind it. But this was relatively minor compared to the attention of ufologists and crop circles researchers, predictably certain that the only way such a shape could have appeared was as some kind of message from outer space. After all, who else would have put it where only birdlife was likely to see it, and for what reason?

Unlike today's circlemakers, who see art in people's responses to circles, as far as Doug Bower was concerned his artistic bent was satisfied by painting, whereas the circles represented his otherworldly fantasies; after years of fantasising about flying saucers, who else was going to realise them but him? Meanwhile, Doug's successors have taken his vision to its logical extreme, operating from the chaotic fringe of logic and reason – the grey area from where myths stream, creativity blooms and phenomena evolve.

The most common argument against crop circle making is "Why bother?" As

THE FIELD GUIDE

Brian Eno has observed:

> *A way of doing something original is by trying something so painstaking that nobody else has ever bothered with it... Then the question arises in the mind: Why are they going to all this trouble? I like this question. I like any question that makes you start thinking about the "outside" of the experience – because it makes the experience bigger.*

The essence of this playful interaction with supernatural phenomena is that it creates elaborate form out of disconnected myths, from which new truths may emerge. By engaging with it we participate in a theatre of creativity, in which to escape convention. We don't necessarily have to either believe in, or reject, the phenomena to gain from the vision. By presenting us with unexpected novelty, which threatens, cajoles and ultimately ridicules blind belief (as well as its twin, blind scepticism) we learn new ways to perceive it.

CASE STUDY: THE OLIVERS CASTLE VIDEO FOOTAGE

At approximately 5am on 11 August 1996, crop circle enthusiast John Wheyleigh filmed something extraordinary at Olivers Castle, near Devizes in Wiltshire. He had spent much of that summer staking out potential crop circle locations with his Hi-8 video camera, hoping to capture the elusive circlemaking force in action. And now he had it.

Art and Philosophy

Wheyleigh's shaky 12-second video shows four luminescent spheres or balls of light (BOLs) swooping into frame and circling over a virgin wheat field. As they swirl and dive, the wheat crop beneath them collapses into a relatively simple six-fold, snowflake-shaped crop circle. After a matter of seconds, the BOLs exit stage left, their morning's work done.

Here, at last, was what the circles enthusiasts had spent years hoping for: demonstrable evidence that the crop formations were the work of a mysterious, non-human force. The footage caused a sensation and was screened all over the world, appearing in high-quality TV documentaries including *Strange But True*, *Sighting*s, *Strange Universe* and *The World's Best UFO Footage*. It was analysed by specialists, including Hollywood special effects expert Bruce Logan, whose production credits include *2001: A Space Odyssey*, *Star Wars,* and *Star Trek*. Bruce said of the footage: "Yes, it's possible that this video was produced by man. But only a handful of people in the world would be capable of such work. I think it is extremely unlikely that this is not genuine." Prominent crop circle researcher Michael Glickman has referred to the video as one of "the most important pieces of footage in the world".

However, the truth behind the footage is somewhat more prosaic than the circles enthusiasts would like to believe.

The crop circle depicted in the Olivers Castle video was created during the night

THE FIELD GUIDE

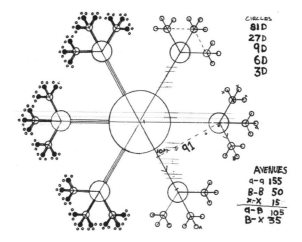

CIRCLES
81 D
27 D
9 D
6 D
3 D

AVENUES
9–9 155
B–B 50
X–X 15
9–B 105
B–X 35

Diagram used *to create the Olivers Castle crop circle.*

of 10th August 1996 by a team of three circlemakers. The choice of the *Mission Impossible* film soundtrack to accompany their drive from London to Wiltshire that evening was, in retrospect, apt. Construction of the circle started later than hoped, as what seemed from the hilltop to be a straightforward set of fields to navigate through became labyrinthine come nightfall, especially when approached from the wrong direction. Consequently the formation put down in the field was less complex than originally intended.

The circlemakers had decided to create, for the first time, a design whose radiating arms were not enclosed by a ring (such rings serve as an aid to construction) – this, they hoped, would provide another pointer to its non-human origins. The team had also decided that this would be a good opportunity to try out Doug Bower's pioneering method of constructing straight lines freehand, using a cap with a sighting mechanism attached, as sported by Doug in the *Today* newspaper photographs.

Unfortunately the decision proved to be a shortsighted one. The night was too dark to identify objects on the horizon to aim towards, so construction of the six arms of the formation took much longer than anticipated. Viewed from the air, one of the arms is decidedly lopsided. Comparing the actual formation to the original construction diagram one sees that there should also have been more fractal details on each arm. Of course, as the intended audience would never have the luxury of seeing the original design, they would be none-the-wiser about the formation's shortcomings.

The circlemakers exited the field as the sun's rays began to appear on the horizon. Their part in the creation of the Olivers Castle footage was complete. Now came phase two.

The cameraman's real name was John Wabe and he worked at 1st Cut Digital Post Production Studios in Bristol, which had recently taken delivery of a Silicon Graphics "Flame" effects studio. One of the features in the software's box of tricks was the ability to add camera shake to previously stable footage. The wobbly "hand held" Hi-8 camerawork of the Olivers Castle video is all digital: the crop circle was actually shot using a large, professional DigiBeta camera mounted on a tripod.

When planning the footage, its creators knew that the time window between when the footage was shot and when it was first screened would be crucial to its being accepted as authentic by the circles enthusiasts. John shot the footage of the circle at daybreak, then drove to Bristol to work his digital wizardry. He then returned to the Barge Inn in Alton Barnes, Wiltshire – a mecca for crop circle seekers – and screened the footage that same evening to a rapt audience. It was a job well done. The footage has since gone down in UFO and crop circles history, and is considered to be amongst the "best evidence" for the mysterious origins of both phenomena.

The Olivers Castle case presents us with a fine example of ostension in action, where gaps in ongoing mythology are soon filled, often by artists responding to ambient desire. Long standing rumours that balls of light were behind the formations were transformed into documentary fact thanks to the ingenuity of the circlemaking team and their collaborator, not to mention some hard work and (then) state-of-the-art computer software.

Circles enthusiast *Polly Carson (left) and friend watch the Olivers Castle footage.*

THE BEGINNERS' GUIDE:
ROLL YOUR OWN

THE FIELD GUIDE

Although the essence of the magic of the circles phenomenon lies in its covert manufacture, we strongly suggest that you seek permission from landowners before flattening their crop – criminal damage is a punishable offence!

When moving around the fields please use public rights of way. Do not damage property, environment or wildlife. Take your equipment and litter home with you.

It is important to remember that crop circles exist in an atmosphere of faith. If you create circles you share a responsibility to respect the rites and beliefs that surround the phenomenon.

THE CANVAS

Circles have appeared worldwide in wheat, oats, spinach, grass, peas, linseed, maize, oil-seed rape, sunflowers, mustard, barley, sugar-beet, rye, and a multitude of other crops. Circlemakers tend to concentrate on just three: oil-seed rape, barley and wheat. These are grown and harvested in a smooth, overlapping progression, the first in April through May, the second throughout May and June, the latter from June until early September.

Roll Your Own

From left to right...
wheat, barley and oats

Know Your Crop

In the UK, crop circles can be made in a variety of crops throughout the growing season of April to August. Good crop recognition skills and a full knowledge of crop types are an essential to any circle maker.

Much of southern England is peppered with huge grain fields - a consequence of modern farming and contrasting greatly to the Neolithic sites that are abundant in the area.

Crop circles are mostly made in cereal crop and rape seed. Here we concentrate on the most popular of these materials.

THE FIELD GUIDE

Grass

Theoretically crop circles can be made as early as March in long grass, such as the above example in Avebury, Wiltshire. Grass markings have an even longer history than cereal markings. In UFO lore, grass markings have been interpreted as the landing marks of unknown craft for at least the last 40 years.

> *Example: A classic case was presented to the American public in 1974 by Terrence Mitchell, a Minnesota investigator who had noted a set of mysterious series of circles in Meeker County. The aerial photographs of the circles were promoted by Linda Moulton-Howe, a TV journalist and cattle mutilation researcher. Apparent cattle mutilations were found in the vicinity of the circles, lending a sinister atmosphere that both researchers exploited in their public presentations*

and TV appearances. After Mitchell appeared on a TV news show
further investigations into the circles found that they were actually
snow covered silage. By 1975 Mitchell had recanted the UFO link
and by 1992 Linda Moulton-Howe had refocused her research and
joined the annual pilgrimage of international tourists to view the
circlemakers' work.

The grass circles of UFO lore share many cultural features of fairy or fungi rings. Fungi or Toadstool rings are caused by the distribution of underground mycelium causing the grass to discolour in roughly circular areas.

Oil Seed Rape or Canola

From late April to early May rape fields flower with bright almost sulphur yellow petals. The plants grow to at least five feet tall and have thick green brittle stems.

For many circlemakers flowering rape is the first call of the season to the fields. Circles in rape can look absolutely stunning, but making them can be hard slog in the cold and wet – at night the temperature can drop to 0°C.

Generally there is only a short time window once the plant has flowered before it becomes too tangled to make neat designs. Within two weeks or so the plant sheds its flowers, and circle making becomes very difficult.

The height of the plants and difficulty in flattening them without damaging the stems tends to restrict the designs that are placed in rape fields.

Perhaps the best design in a rape field was placed next to Silbury Hill, Wiltshire. The Beltane Wheel of 1998 *(right)* was created on the night of the pagan festival of Beltane. Measuring some 200ft across and composed mainly of rings this was still relatively small compared to many formations in other crops.

Barley

This is a thin fragile plant, growing to around three feet. The heads of the barley plant sprout a rasping feather-like head. Ripening barley (from late May onwards) droops as it dries producing a kink just below the seed head. Consequently, barley circles tend to have a soft appearance without the hard "cookie cutter" edge that is normally associated with wheat crop circles.

Barley is a bright green colour and while the plant is ripening it is extremely supple and will start to recover from any circle making activity quite quickly. This produces

Roll Your Own

A circle *in ripe barley one day after creation: note the lumpiness of the lay as the plants recover back towards the light, a process known as phototropism.*

some curious effects as the plant continues to grow upwards with a permanent bend in its stem from the residue of the flattening process.

These effects, of course, are seen as a classic trait of the genuine phenomenon. It is argued that no human flattening process could produce such delicate results. While it may be frustrating to see your handiwork virtually disappear in a day, remember you are contributing to one of the true hallmarks of the crop circle phenomenon.

It is still possible to make circles in mature barley, but you will find the stems buckle creating a messy and unappealing lay to your design.

THE FIELD GUIDE

Oats

Oats present a loose arrangement of seeds attached to branches that spring out from the central stem of the crop. Standing at about the same height as wheat and barley, while it is possible to make circles in oats they do have a tendency to appear rather soft, much like barley. Annually, very few circles are created in oats.

Wheat

From late June and early July wheat will be ripe enough to make crisp flat designs. The crop is favoured by the best circlemakers, and found extensively in Wiltshire near many ancient sites. In the southern UK, wheat is harvested around the middle of August.

Wheat offers the circlemaker a shimmering canvas to work on. Its strength and straight stem will allow you to create the classic cookie cutter edge to your circle, and an infinite variety of woven lays. From the air flattened mature wheat laid in simple circles appear as shining metallic, and distinctly otherworldly, discs in the landscape.

Roll Your Own

EQUIPMENT

The tools you will need are relatively unsophisticated: a 300ft surveyors tape (this is preferable to string which tends to tangle easily), a one-to-two metre board or plank with a rope at each end to form a loop (this is known as a stalk-stomper), dowsing rods (preferably copper and vastly overpriced, available in any New Age retailer, but in an emergency two bent coat hangers will do) and an optional plastic garden roller. A luminous watch is also useful as a summer night can be surprisingly brief.

Tape measures should be of the white cloth variety with measurements marked in black – the type marked in red will require a torch to read in the dark. Tapes can be linked together with clips to make lengths longer than 300ft.

The Stalk Stomper

Developed by Doug Bower in about 1980, the stomper consists of a board about one metre long and usually around one inch thick. A length of rope is threaded through holes at either end of the board. The rope is then held in the hands, while one foot rests on the board.

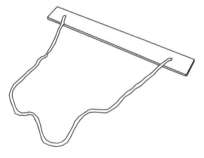

THE FIELD GUIDE

Other developments on the stomper's basic design have included wider boards (up to seven inches) giving a more stable foot platform and most notoriously a double length plank (dubbed robostomper) which was bolted together once in the field, allowing two metre swathes of crop to be flattened. The stomper suffers from one particular limitation; it is not the best implement for flattening oil seed rape (tall yellow flowering crops). The oil-seed rape, or canola plant (as it is known in the US), is extremely brittle and breaks easily when flattened. Even rounded edges on your stomper won't reduce plant breakages, or prevent tell-tale scuff marks on the stems of the plants. For working in oil seed rape we recommend either using rollers (which severely limits the size of the formation you can create) or covering your stomper with foam and gaffer tape to make it cushion the plants as they are pushed over. Either of these options present their own problems and oil seed rape is notoriously difficult to work with, even with the right equipment. It is for this reason that circles made in this medium are smaller and less complex than those that appear in wheat or barley.

The stomper has been the circlemakers favoured flattening implement since the early 1980s. Other implements have been used but with less success. Jim Schnabel and Rob Irving popularised the use of garden rollers in the early 1990s. While a roller creates a smooth lay, and can be hired inexpensively from tool hire shops, its relatively narrow width (two feet) and bulkiness make it impractical for concealing in the boot of your car, or moving around the countryside discreetly.

Roll Your Own

To use the stomper, grasp the loop of rope in each hand as if you are holding horses' reins. Make sure you hold the rope high enough so as not to cause you to stoop. Rest the stomper on the ground and place your leading foot at the centre of the board. Flattening the crop is simply a matter of lifting the stomper with your leading foot and taking a large step into the standing crop, illustrated above. Now bring your trailing foot up to the stomper and repeat the process. You will leave a swathe of beautifully flattened crop in your wake.

Clothing

It is important to wear warm clothing and good walking shoes, carry waterproof trousers and bring plenty of drinking water. Circlemaking is often physical, hard work and may dehydrate you.

THE FIELD GUIDE

Despite balmy summer evenings the nights can get surprisingly cold and damp. Any moisture on the crop will guarantee you will be wet from the waist down for several hours.

Apart from travelling to and from the site, during the production of a large pattern you can expect to walk several miles. One person flattening a circle 100ft across using a four foot stomper will require legwork over approximately 1.5 miles.

NB The traditional menacing black garb of the circle maker is now largely symbolic, although a drab appearance has obvious practical benefits.

LOCATION

Choose your site depending on:

a/ Visibility. A field rising from the road, or an amphitheatre in full view of a road, make perfect circles sites. Remember, if you are in a field visible from the road you may be visible too. While car drivers will not be able to see you because their eyes are adjusted to the headlights, cyclists and walkers are very likely to see or hear you.

b/ Symbolism. Many circlemakers choose to work adjacent to or in alignment with ancient sacred sites, particularly those from the Neolithic period. These are to be

Roll Your Own

found throughout the UK. The extra effort in finding such a site will be returned by the added layers of mystery poured on it. Such sites also offer attractive opportunities for aerial photography, particularly if the geometry of the crop pattern echoes that of the ancient monument.

c/ Access. Some fields offer quick access by way of convenient parking locations or well-trodden footpaths. If you think your pattern is going to take a whole night to construct, pick a field that has good access and a handy exit. Remember, if you found the field easy to enter others will too; a circlemaker's worst nightmare is a stranger entering the field unnoticed while the circle is being made.

d/ Remoteness. Some circlemakers prefer to work in remote areas unpopulated by either sacred sites or cerealogists (known collectively as croppies). While benefits are obvious, one possible drawback is that the pattern may not be found or viewed by anyone other than the driver of the combine harvester mowing it down.

Once the location and design have been decided, retire to a local pub and wait for twilight. If the location is in a well known circles-prone area, such as Alton Barnes in Wiltshire, you may be able to pick up some useful intelligence on the plans of the croppies. They are usually very public about their intentions, and generous in providing information on their own viewpoints, hideouts and equipment (night vision etc).

THE FIELD GUIDE

It is not advisable to socialise with croppies, however, as conversation invariably deteriorates to inwardly spiralling argument which will eat into the time you have allotted to circlemaking. This might lead to a smaller pattern, therefore defeating the object of your argument.

Dowsing

Naturally, you will have organised your design to incorporate earth energies or "ley" lines. This can require expertise as the lines snake and resonate as they synchronise with the pulse of the Universe. Dowse the potential site to establish the strongest current, noting its direction. If a pattern is located on a powerful energy line this will satisfy initial tests for genuineness, and aid in curative effects, orgone accumulation, angelic visions, benign alien abduction experiences and general feelings of well-being.

Warning: A pattern situated contra-directionally to the flow of energy may cause the opposite effects: headaches, nausea, temporary paralysis, aching limbs and joints, mental illness, over-exposure to deadly orgone radiation (DOR), demonic visions, malignant alien abduction scenarios (memory loss, implant scarring, sore or bleeding anus, navel, genitals etc) and feelings of disillusionment. The authors have noted with neutrality that this may be of interest to Satanists.

Roll Your Own

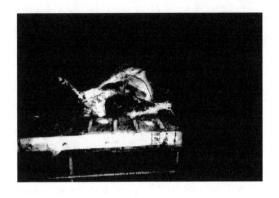

Investigators *who found this mutilated sheep were unable to determine whether it had suffered at the hands of deranged perverts or strayed into the contra-flow of a powerful ley line.*

The Drop Off

After making sure that you have not been followed from the pub, drive to the field and unload any equipment that cannot be easily carried in a pocket or rucksack. Be careful to leave it in a place that you can recognise in darkness – a gate or large bush, for instance. Then drive to a sensible parking place. Remember that an empty vehicle may arouse suspicion if it is left in a lay-by or farm track, or by the side of the field. Our advice is to park in the nearest village with other cars, then quietly and invisibly walk to the field.

You will have already decided in your planning precisely where in the field to begin your pattern. Move to this point using the relevant "tram", or tractor line. Do not move through a crop field without using the tramlines – criminal damage is a serious offence.

Ritual

Before commencing the work, a simple ritual should be performed. This will assist in causing minimal damage on a quantum level while the stalks are being laid. Using a long, curved, razor-sharp blade, cut seven single stalks for every circle planned for the formation. Place each one between the thumb and forefinger and stroke until the stem starts to bend. When all the stems are bent at a 45° about two inches from their base, place each sheaf at the centre of its corresponding circle as you go along. If this service is not performed, a greater ratio of breakage will occur. Cerealogists who find a sheaf of sharply cut stems within a crop circle tend to automatically see this as a sign of genuineness.

One well-known circlemaker practices a variation of the above, fashioning his sheaf into human form and placing the dolly into the final circle to ensure future good fortune.

Fig 1

THE CIRCLE

Establish the centre of your first circle about six feet from the tram-line, walking with an angled, loping stride that will not leave an obvious path to the centre (*Fig. 1*).

Roll Your Own

Make the centre by turning on an axis of your standing foot whilst dragging the crop down with the other. An attractive nested centre can be fashioned by hand – this will lend more evidence of genuineness and increase the likelihood of positive results in any subsequent microbiological study. Alternately, use a stomper or a roller – individual circlemakers can develop their own style of centre as a subtle signature.

Gradually move outwards to create a circle about one metre across. At this point you may wish to create a false centre – simply mark an axis for the larger circle elsewhere - or even a second or third centre. All these attributes are recognised signs of genuineness.

172

The Perimeter

You are now ready to form the perimeter of your circle. If you are working alone, place a barbecue stick (or similar) in or near the centre, attaching your tape through the loop. If working plurally, one of you will act as the axis, holding the end of the tape high and close to the chest, thus preventing the tape from dragging the standing crop. The other will measure out the radius of the circle by walking away from the centre, preferably along a tram-line rather than through standing crop (*Fig. 2*).

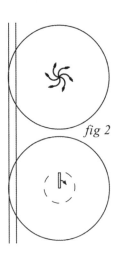

fig 2

Then, take up the slack and step sideways and continue on into the standing crop leaving a narrow but visible trail until you return to your starting point. Keep your eyes on the centre at all times and keep the tape taught.

NB: At certain angles a breeze may cause the tape to vibrate and make a loud whooping noise. Do not be alarmed; Under scientific analysis this sound has been identified as an authenticating mark of the true circle maker.

Flow and Multiple Layering

You are now ready to roll or stomp the rest of the circle. A circle flattened from **173** the inside out will produce what is known as a radial lay, as termed by cerealogists Colin Andrews and Pat Delgado in earlier times when Doug and Dave had few emulators – the radial lay was the latter's speciality. The reverse – working from the outside towards the centre – will result in a near concentric spiral, "like water". Naturally, both of these effects are regarded as genuine and consistent with the non-man-made ethos.

The same can be said of almost any artefact of construction. The wide latitude experts offer to evidence of authenticity allows the circlemaker great freedom of expression. Circles, crescents, rings, arcs and aisles, insects, webs and fractals... there are myriad ideas and symbols that you can incorporate into your design, as long – a general rule of thumb – as it does not suggest a direct relationship with Man. Anthropomorphism is best projected, rather than reflected.

Baffling complexity will always be popular amongst croppies. But, while it is the authors' ideal that the bread belt be filled with a Zen aesthetic, we concede that this is a matter of taste. We hope, however, that you will apply some deftness to the merging of these elements.

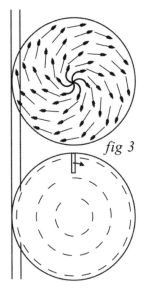

fig 3

Your stomper is a tool that, if used carefully, can create the most intricate of woven lays and reverse flows, and much delight for the admirer.

Figure 3 shows you how to create a spiral lay. First, rotate the stomper once around the centre of the circle. Continue gradually moving out to the perimeter – the tightness of the swirl depends upon the angle and direction at which you approach the perimeter. Note that as you move concentrically around the centre the crop splays out radially. It is possible to accentuate this attractive feature by angling the stomper slightly outwards.

THE FIELD GUIDE

Grapeshot

Even the most dogmatic of cerealogists now consider grapeshot (*above*) – small circles, usually about three feet across, separate from the main pattern, often in the form of a signature – to be man-made. Normally such concession precedes widespread dismissal as a genuine component. Discretion is advised.

Noise Levels

At night in an open landscape, we are more sensitive to sound than during the day. We can discern people talking from 500ft away – likewise, they can hear us. If you are working in a group keep noise to a minimum, whispering whenever possible. Do not attempt to issue forth across the span of a large pattern. Move in close proximity of the person you want to communicate with.

Roll Your Own

You may feel that stomping or rolling the crop also exceeds acceptable noise levels. Whilst it may be heard several hundred feet away it is usually interpreted as a rhythmic natural sound and is unlikely to arouse suspicion.

Be generally wary of anyone: campers and tourists, farm workers, occultists, badger hunters, nocturnal dog walkers etc.

Geometric Complexity

There are few substitutes for complex and meaningful geometric relationships in your design. Much of crop circles research has evolved to focus on this, as if, perhaps, otherworldly secrets can be translated through mathematics. This is of course particularly relevant to sacred geometry or any contemplation of divisions of the circle or circular mandala.

The following diagrams reveal the sequence used to construct a pattern opposite the Avebury stone circle in July 1999. A six-fold hexagonal structure, it measured 300ft in diameter and utilised sacred geometry, isometric projections and optical illusion. While somewhat complex, it demonstrates what is possible to create in four-and-a-half hours with a small team of circlemakers.

THE FIELD GUIDE

The Avebury Triangle

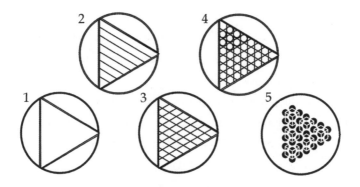

Roll Your Own

Sequence of construction:

1/   An equilateral triangle inscribed in a circle.

2/   At fixed points along each side of the triangle an isometric grid is created by stretching a tape from point to point and carefully walking along it, leaving a narrow trail through the crop.

3/   This procedure is repeated across the three axes of the triangle...

4/   ...creating an isometric grid composed of 33 hexagons.

5/   Each hexagon is then inscribed with a circle. Each of the 33 circles serves as a component for the final projected cubes.

The sides of each of the cubes are flattened from the centre of the circle to a corner of the hexagon (*right*). Each circle requires a different set of cube sides to be flattened to create the isometrically projected cubes.

Finally the area around both the circles and the triangles is flattened leaving the circles as standing columns of crop with the cube sides flattened into each circle.

The formation was commissioned by the *Daily Mail* newspaper. Despite publicity of this fact, experts claimed it is one of the most complex of non-man-made patterns.

The Sunflower

Woodborough Hill, *Wilts August 2000 – approximately 250ft in diameter with over 300 individually flattened segments.*

The Woodborough Hill formation held a classic geometric imprint of various natural forms, such as a sunflower seed head and a pine cone. This template is created through interlocking Fibonacci spirals, natural growth spirals that are modelled using a simple mathematical sequence. The Fibonacci curve is also a proto-fractal – self-similar at any point along its curvature.

The Moiré Ring

The Moiré *near Avebury, Wilts July 2000 – approximately 240ft across with over 350 individual standing segments.*

This pattern resembling optically dynamic moiré rings was laid down two miles from Avebury henge. It was constructed from a series of 120 radiating straight lines that converge at 60 equidistant points. The convergence and intersections create the chequer pattern. Every alternate chequer has been flattened, creating this mind-boggling design.

The Temple

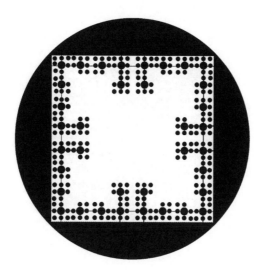

Windmill Hill, *Wilts, July 1999 – approximately*
320ft across with over 280 separate circles.

Laid down near a sacred Neolithic site, the geometry of this pattern is based on a set of nested invisible squares which repeat in iterations. Each underlying square proportionately decreased in size creating a geometry clearly related to non-linear, or fractal mathematical theories. Many thought the formation resembled the ground plan of a temple.

The Grid

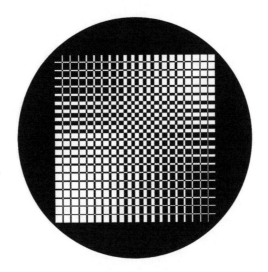

East Kennet, Wilts, *July 2000 – approximately 200ft in diameter with 1600 individually flattened elements.*

Situated in the heart of crop circle country, this grid appears to be optically shifting from dark to light and vice-versa. The lay comprised of bands of crop woven between the standing clumps. Still one of the most complex crop circles to date, it prompted a flurry of media reports soon after its appearance.

Sacred Geometry

Throughout history and across cultures, the circular mandala has been attributed cosmological significance. It is extensively used in religious iconography both in the West and the East. Underlying sacred geometry provides a powerful set of psychological metaphors that can be utilised to express and stimulate a rich set of interpretations.

Aside from religious applications, capitalism with its reflexive and adaptable mechanisms has tried to absorb the lessons of sacred geometry, for instance with the Mercedes logo – a circle divided into a trinity.

For the circlemaker this type of geometry has a practical function as well as a symbolic one. All sacred geometrical forms are constructed from the divisions created by the intersection of arcs and circles.

For example, it is possible to inscribe a hexagon inside a circle using one measurement. The radius of the circle is exactly the same size as the length of the side of the hexagon that will inscribe the circle. By virtue of its inherent symmetry sacred geometry involves much repetition in construction. This too aids the circle maker. Multiple acts of repetition are very easily and efficiently carried out in the field.

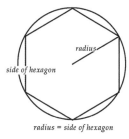

radius = side of hexagon

Roll Your Own

Symbology

The gods we create interact with us through symbols. Just as they are continuous with people, so our relationship with them is continuous with other human systems, such as art and science, as a means of interpreting and influencing our existence. It would be hard to find a more literal example of this than crop patterns.

The symbology of sacred geometry lends the circles much of their cosmological significance. Proportions generated by circle-based geometry are found across the natural world.

Our genes are carried by the very particular double helix geometry of DNA. In space gigantic spiral universes mirror the geometry found in growth spirals in plants. Dendritic patterns are formed on huge scale in river beds and deltas, and carry the very same branching structure found in many trees and other foliage.

The Fibonacci sequence, represented by a mathematical equation, is extraordinary in formulation; self-similar at any point in its curvature. It is found across many natural forms, and when not visually present its mathematical sequence controls the growth patterns of many organic forms.

Example: The Julia Set at Stonehenge, 1996 (*opposite*). The pattern consisted of 151 individual circles arranged in a huge spiral, with circles decreasing in size along its curvature. Smaller spirals branched off from the main pattern, creating a fractal-like design.

Roll Your Own

Likewise, snowflakes are composed around variants of a hexagonal, or six-fold structure. Each snowflake carries this geometric imprint and is also unique in its own particular details. There is also much evidence that land markings in previous eras have also incorporated the use of similar geometry. Stonehenge is widely thought to be a lunar and solar observatory which deploys the necessary geometry in its structure to use it to make predictions of the movement of the heavens, lunar eclipses etc. It seemed an appropriate place to host such a symbolic crop circle.

In time and with practice you will learn how to explore the geometry touched upon here and your circles will begin to satisfy the spiritual and religious needs of those that visit them.

THE FIELD GUIDE

CASE STUDY:BBC *A PICTURE OF BRITAIN* FORMATION

The Circlemakers were asked to produce a crop circle as part of the BBC art series *A Picture of Britain,* presented by David Dimbleby. The original inspirations for our piece were the optical illusion paintings – known as "Op Art" – created by artists such as Bridget Riley and Victor Varsley. These artists use optical illusions to create paintings that make the retina vibrate and the brain struggle to interpret the images as they appear to shift and change in front of you in puzzling and apparently impossible ways. This makes them an ideal form for rendering The Circlemakers' aim of creating seemingly impossible feats of design and construction, and so pushing the limits of what is deemed to be humanly possible in the field.

187

The first crop circle to use such optical devices appeared opposite Avebury Avenue in July 1999. It was commissioned by the *Daily Mail* newspaper, who wanted us to demonstrate our craft. The design we created used the "impossible triangle" motif rendered as a series of six three-dimensional cubes, as originally conceived by Roger Penrose (see *page 176*). That formation was the first of its kind and spawned a whole new family of designs.

The formation for the BBC also incorporated sacred geometry, a key component in the most successful crop circle designs. We used the number Phi (1.61803) – pronounced "fee" – otherwise known as the golden ratio. Phi could be described as the mathematics of nature and has been used by artists including da Vinci, Dali and Vermeer. It appears

188

THE FIELD GUIDE

in an astonishing number of places in nature: mollusc shells, sunflower seed heads, the surface of pineapples, fractals, crystals, in the shapes of galaxies – and in a number of crop circle designs.

Our brief was to create a design that incorporated the optical qualities of Op Art while being underpinned by sacred geometry. Using the original Op Art design (*opposite*) we used a simple piece of sacred geometry that is called squaring the circle. If you draw a square around a circle, then scribe a circle which touches all four corners of the square, the ratio of the two circles is equal to Phi.

That we were to be a crew of only four put a natural cap on the complexity of the design, so the number of individual segments was reduced from 80 to a more manageable 20, while still keeping the diameter of the crop circle at an impressive 300ft. One of the design iterations reflected a stained glass Rose window that the team had recently seen in Milan's Duomo Cathedral, adding an unexpected extra layer of possible meaning and interpretation.

The key to a successful crop circle design is visual complexity that is actually built upon relatively simple, repeatable geometric elements. Visually the BBC design reads as a series of overlapping clockwise and counterclockwise logarithmic Fibonacci curves; these would be extremely difficult to construct accurately under cover of darkness in five hours. In fact, the curves are made up of several identical sub elements, criss-crossing

Roll Your Own

straight lines constructed inside each of the twenty segments. Although still visually complex these are much simpler to construct, and because the elements in each segment are identical, the construction process is reasonably swift.

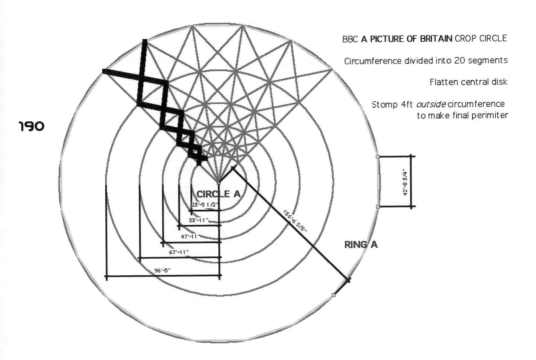

BBC **A PICTURE OF BRITAIN** CROP CIRCLE

Circumference divided into 20 segments

Flatten central disk

Stomp 4ft *outside* circumference
to make final perimiter

CIRCLE A

23'-5 1/2"

33'-11"

47'-11"

67'-11"

96'-5"

42'-9 3/4"

135'-9 5/8"

RING A

THE FIELD GUIDE

The construction process, deconstructed

Fig 1. (overleaf) The first phase of creating the crop circle was the construction of CIRCLE A, a 47ft diameter circle. We then scribed a 272ft diameter ring (RING A) around it, with a four foot wide path around the outside of the ring.

Fig 2. Next we divided RING A into 4 segments, marking them with a pole every 214ft, then subdivided these four sections into twenty segments, placing a pole in the ground every 42' 8".

Fig 3. Next we prepared two pieces of twine that both measured 136' 6", the radius from the centre of CIRCLE A to the inside edge of RING A. We attached gaffer tape at the following measurements 23' 5", 33' 11", 47' 11", 67' 11", 96' 5". These correspond to the radii of the squared circle rings that were on the original diagram. Where each inferred ring meets the twine is a construction point; note that we never actually scribe any of these rings. Next we set up the two pieces of twine, stretching them both from the centre of CIRCLE A to the first two segments tying the twine to poles that mark each point.

Fig 4. We then constructed two zigzagging lines that weave from left to right between the two pieces of twine, connecting up the gaffer tape markers. Starting at RING A one of the crew took a tape measure and in loping steps – so as not to leave a trace – heading diagonally through the standing crop towards the first gaffer tape marker. Once there the

Roll Your Own

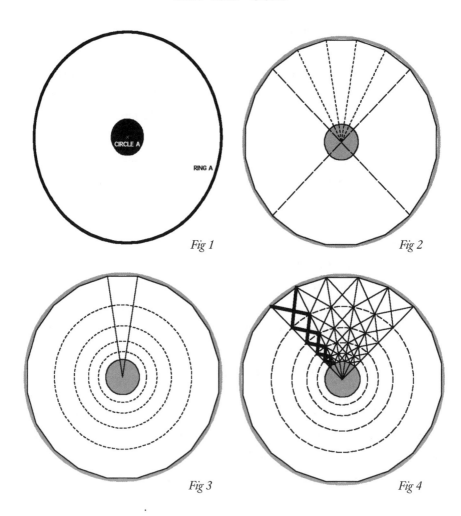

Fig 1

Fig 2

Fig 3

Fig 4

THE FIELD GUIDE

tape was pulled tight and a second crew member created a foot-line along the tape by walking sideways through the crop, dragging their feet so as to leave a flattened one-foot-wide path in the crop. Finally a third crew member stomped along the foot-line, making sure to keep the stomper straddling the middle of the line, aided by a white mark in the centre of the board. This process was repeated 20 times. The final part of construction was to widen the external ring by stomping one more time around the circumference of the earlier flattened ring.

It was only later that we realised the startling similarity between the crop circle we'd created for the BBC and the design of the Piazza del Campidoglio in Rome, Italy (*overleaf*) which has a twelve-pointed flower laid out on the ground designed by Michaelangelo. Cosmic coincidence in action!

Roll Your Own

THE FIELD GUIDE

COCK UPS

Even the most experienced circlemakers make mistakes - flatten over a perimeter, misalign a design element, etc.

If you find yourself in this situation try to rectify it by changing the design and flattening other areas to reinstall some symmetry to the altered design. If necessary, flatten a circle over the whole design to cover any bad errors. While this may be upsetting, remember that you are the only person that is aware of the original design, and if you alter it no-one else will know.

Moreover, do not forget that any "ghost" or underlying construction lines from the original plan will be regarded by experts as tangible proof that the circle is not man-made.

Do not leave a pattern unfinished because it has mistakes in it. If you are forced to leave, and return later to complete the job be aware of the obvious risk; you may literally stumble upon devoted croppies, perhaps sleeping or performing rituals. The authors once discovered to his alarm that what at first appeared as a curiously ambiguous "luminosity" at the centre of the circle turned out to be New Age couple gazing into the night sky and observing the universe revolve around them.

Roll Your Own

EXIT & DETRITUS

Bear in mind that you will probably leave the site exhausted; in the early hours your blood sugar levels will be at their lowest and it is easy to lose concentration. Before leaving the site, always check that you have not left anything behind.

Sweet wrappers, cigarette butts, empty beer cans, string… whilst not always regarded by cerealogists as signs of human involvement, they may create extra work for early-bird researchers. For example, we have observed string being found at a fresh site and secretly pocketed by one well-known cerealogist.

Michael Green, Chairman of the Centre for Crop Circle Studies once found a stalk-stomper in a circle – it had been covered by the flattened crop – but identified it as a "measuring stick" and quickly mislaid it elsewhere in the field.

On another famous occasion, revealed at the CCCS annual conference in 1993, Sussex-based researcher Barry Reynolds found a broken stomper in a circle. He told the audience that he had no idea what the object was, but wondered whether it could be an important piece of evidence. After its likely use had been explained and demonstrated on stage, Reynolds then speculated that it was dropped by helicopter, immediately after the circle was discovered, as part of a government-sponsored disinformation campaign.

THE FIELD GUIDE

NIGHT VISION, AUTOKINESIS & BLIND SPOTS

Flashlights are not a part the circle maker's kit-bag, so you will have to rely on your own night vision. Learn to trust it, but only to a point. In the dark your pupils increasingly dilate over a period of an hour or so to absorb the ambient light. It is surprising how much light there is on a moonlight night. Sometimes it may feel like too much; on a clear night with a full moon you will cast a shadow across the crop, and white tape or diagrams will seem particularly luminous. Don't worry, it would be hard for observers to see you, especially if you are situated between them and the moon (usually approximately to the south in the UK). Looking at the moon they will be able to see far less than you, who will be looking away from the moon. The authors have made crop circles in full moonlight knowing that we were being surveilled from a short distance away by so-called "hoaxbusters" armed with night-vision equipment – we could see them clearly, but we knew they couldn't see us.

Two main factors impair your vision whilst circlemaking. Both are effects of an absence of light on your optical system. They can induce near hallucinations and paranoia.

Because of the eye's physiology, in darkness it is sometimes harder to identify objects directly in front of you: they will appear more clearly defined on the edge or periphery of your vision. In such a circumstance we can see some objects only when we

Roll Your Own

look away from them. This can often lead to an impression the object is moving. While it makes good evolutionary sense for our peripheral vision to be more sensitive to light and movement, our Great Designer had probably not envisaged that it would create problems for cereal artists (as well as astronomers, N-ray discoverers and ufologists).

While a modicum of paranoia is useful in the field, do not become overly alarmed if bushes and trees suddenly become people. It has been known for whole teams of circle-makers to evacuate a field, one of them having been chased by a fence post.

The eye also constructs illusions around isolated objects, particularly bright objects in the sky without any useful frame of reference. Because our eyes are constantly building up a fragmented picture, unreferenced stationary objects can appear to flit about our field of vision. This is commonly known as the "bumble bee" effect.

It may not be the objects themselves, or even light playing tricks on us, but our own perceptions aided by inherent design imperfection.

The countryside can be a strange and noisy place at night. Expect to hear some discomforting sounds. The most worrying we have heard (apart from the sound of other humans) is a fox call – it sounds like a baby screaming blue murder.

THE FIELD GUIDE

UFOs, IFOs & ANOMALOUS LIGHTS

In the unlikely but possible scenario that you witness some kind of strange aerial phenomenon whilst making a circle, try to keep your mind on the job. Summer nights are short enough without distractions. Concentration will conquer your fear. If you are with a friend, check that they saw or heard the disturbance too.

Be aware of possible IFOs (Identified Flying Objects) that can look disconcerting in the murky darkness of the country at night. These include: planes (they always have at least one flashing light), parachute flares, satellites (characterised by slow and steady movement across the sky) and celestial phenomena such as the Moon and Venus.

Of course it is always possible that you are witnessing another artist's work. Favoured methods for this type of activity include balloons with small lights inside them, and high powered disco lights located on a hill.

Sadly it is most likely that your perceptions (which are particularly paranoid and unreliable whilst circlemaking and can induce autokinetic illusions, like those just described) have been tricked by something mundane like an atmospheric effect. This will happen at some point in your circlemaking experience. However, three dramatic sightings are recounted below that may well have had an anomalous origin.

Roll Your Own

Example 1: from Julian Richardson

Towards the end of the 1992 season our circlemaking team decided to test our refined techniques by attempting to produce what was, at the time probably the most complicated design ever. It was while creating that formation that the following event occurred:

As the sky grew darker we slowly walked along the narrow footpath that ran alongside our intended canvas. I knew we had to start early if we had any chance of completing the formation before daybreak. Once

THE FIELD GUIDE

*in the field our initial job was to set up the datum line – a taut length
of string (on this occasion pulled diagonally across a number of tram
lines) that acts as a spinal cord from which the formation can grow.
Finally we were off, and like the low munching of sheep our stompers began
to turn the design into reality. After about an hour we three circlemakers
converged on the same point and began quietly discussing our progress.
Suddenly my attention was drawn to a light that had appeared from
nowhere. It was a few hundred yards away and directly in front of us.
As soon as I'd registered its presence I alerted my colleagues. Amazed
we stood there gazing at this football sized orange light as it hung
motionless, about 40 ft above the surrounding countryside. After an
estimated five seconds the light began to slowly descend. Within another
five seconds it had descended about ten ft and had faded into invisibility.
With little time to spare we excitedly returned to our work, always
hopeful of a repeat performance.*

*Subsequent daylight checks revealed no evidence of the light's existence.
That year also saw a large increase in the number of luminosities reported
around circle sites. Did we witness a naturally-occurring phenomenon or
were we really being scanned by the genuine circlemakers?*

Be aware that your experience – an entertaining story – is just that, a

Roll Your Own

story, and in the absence of any reliable evidence you are free to believe the sighting was whatever you want it to be.

Example 2: from Rod Dickinson

Undoubtedly there are some real anomalies haunting our landscape. In one case several years ago a circlemaking team witnessed a high and definite burst of light which descended to the ground in a narrow beam about half a mile from where they were working. It was a clear and still night with good visibility. The brightness of the burst illuminated the field like a flash gun – for a split second – leaving one of the circlemakers with a distinctive metallic taste in his mouth. When the flash came all but one of the team hit the ground, believing they had been caught with people wielding cameras.

In subsequent days the sighting was reported by others who had witnessed it. On other occasions circlemakers have had similar sightings, even with journalists present.

Example 3: from John Lundberg

We'd agreed to let a reporter from a London radio station accompany us

THE FIELD GUIDE

one night as we laid down a crop circle in a field in Wiltshire. Part-way through the construction of the formation, there was a powerful burst of light; we all stopped, looked around, and after a bit of headscratching continued the formation. This was followed soon afterwards by an identical burst of light. I later described the experience as analogous to having a flash gun let off in my face, with the light momentarily blinding. Unfortunately, the journalist's recording equipment was switched off at the time of the flashes, as he was helping us craft the formation.

Later that same week, we were out making another formation in the same area. During its construction in heavy rain, we witnessed a series of bright flashes. Unlike the previous all-encompassing bursts of light, these emanated from behind the bushes at the edge of the field, and were accompanied by a loud crackling noise. We carried on, assuming that it was some kind of electrical equipment, perhaps shorting out due to the heavy rain. I returned to the site in daylight to try and locate the source of the flashes, but found only trees and bushes.

Once more during the same week, we were out circlemaking in the same locale. After four hours in the field, as the formation was nearing completion, I was suddenly overcome by a strong sense of foreboding... shortly followed by a similar burst of light. Not wanting to chance a

Roll Your Own

meeting with the source of the flashes, we left. I decided to make that
my last formation of 1994.

The following year we took another journalist out with us. During our
conversations we described the flashes of light to him, but he initially
seemed unconvinced. This is what he later wrote in his article for The Face
magazine:

"About thirty minutes before, John had turned to me as we were a few
feet away on the outer ring, 'Did you pick out that flash,' he asked,
excitedly. 'No,' I told him, wondering if he was trying to spook me. Ten
minutes later John asked again, nothing. Now I'm pacing the other
side of the ring on my own and I get one. A bright flash that seemed to
emanate from the back of my own retina. From nowhere at all in fact. I
ran to where John is standing. 'You saw that one?' 'Yeah,' I say, though
saw isn't the right word. Ten minutes later I pick up a second."

The moral seems to be if you want to see something weird while making circles,
take a journalist with you!

THE FIELD GUIDE

GENUINENESS

Your crop circle or pattern will be deemed by experts to be the genuine, non-man-made "real thing" if:

a/ You are not caught making it.

b/ Its appearance invites cerealogists to attach some symbolic importance to it that will define their philosophy and go down well with an audience... ie fractal patterns/eco-thanatology etc.

A crop circle or pattern will develop its own unique folklore if:

a/ It is placed in a field which cerealogists later claim to have been watching at the time.

b/ Light or audio phenomena are associated with it.

c/ A close prediction is publicised beforehand. For example, the logo of the Center for the Study of Extraterrestrial Intelligence (CSETI) was claimed by its leadership to have originated this way – it implies concinnity with the circlemakers.

d/ Mysterious material substances, such as iron dust, are found in it, especially if these are scientifically analysed and found to be extraterrestrial.

Roll Your Own

THE MEDIA

Once you have made your mark you will want it to be seen and debated. Remember, if handled sensibly the news and entertainment media can serve as a useful channel for you work.

Simple strategies include:

1/ A good starting point is alerting the news desk of local newspapers and TV stations, either directly or indirectly. Becoming a secret "deep throat" source is a good way of ensuring anonymity and avoiding suspicion through familiarity. One way of getting around this is to have your own column.

2/ An aerial photograph could make the difference between your efforts being featured on the front page as opposed to being lost amongst reports of war and pestilence. Why not plan your location in relation to local airfields and flying clubs, or if you know a willing photographer get him to book a flight in advance to avoid the rush. This also ensures your work is recorded in a pristine state, before being trampled by visitors or mown down by farmers.

3/ Remember journalists are primarily interested in facts. It is perfectly acceptable to exaggerate the scale, quality and uniqueness of your creation (croppies practice this tactic

An interesting *approach to the phenomenon was taken by the* CREATIVE REVIEW, *who documented 1993's designs on their cover without further comment.*

regularly). In the unlikely event that a journalist accurately records your work all is not lost, as this may lead to a further story about shape-shifting crop circles.

4/ In the rare event of a journalist bothering to meet you in person it may be best to assume the role of innocent bystander (eg, "I was walking my dog and it definitely wasn't here yesterday…") or, if you feel confident enough, the role of crop circles expert, speaking in certainties and using the plural to describe yourself ("We do have scientific evidence that shows…" "We are getting closer to a solution…" etc). Once you have taken the leap this is easier than it may at first appear.

5/ Speak in easily-swallowed soundbites: "100 per cent genuine", "The dog wouldn't stop barking in the circle", "We do know that 80 per cent are not man made" "All the stems appear to be bent but not broken", etc.

6/ Arrive back at the location of your circle early the next morning and call a live radio or TV phone-in on your mobile. Excitedly describe how the crop circle is materialising in front of your eyes! (If anyone reported your formation before you made the call both the media and croppies will revise the report to favour your more sensational account.)

7/One tried and tested strategy of media manipulation to accompany your circle is to engineer video footage of your formation being created by super-intelligent forces, in the form of easily-generated light phenomena (*see Art & Philosophy chapter*).

Other more risky strategies include persuading a journalist to come with you when you make the circle. The authors of this publication recommend that you should charge the media organisation substantially for this sort of exposé. In such cases you have a moral duty to alert croppies that this particular event will be subject to a "negative" media report, so they are not publicly humiliated by declaring it genuine.

Congratulations! You are now armed with all the information necessary to start producing your own paranormal spectaculars. See you in the field!

209

Doug Bower

IT'S ONLY FLATTENED CORN

THE FIELD GUIDE

Doug Bower *interviewed by John Lundberg*

I first met Doug Bower in the Percy Hobbs pub in Winchester, Hampshire at an informal gathering of circlemakers back in 1994. We've been friends ever since. It was one of those rare occasions when I came face to face with one of my heroes and they didn't disappoint or undermine my expectations of them.

Doug, along with his partner-in-crime Dave Chorley, can be credited with inventing the crop circle phenomenon as we know it today. Every Friday night they would meet up in the Percy Hobbs pub in Winchester to talk about art, life and whatever else was on their minds.

One summer evening in the mid-1970s, after several pints, Doug had flying saucers on his mind. As they were taking the summers air along a bridle path on the Longwood Estate in Hampshire, Doug recalled an event that made headline news in Australia, where he used to live. Pointing to a nearby wheat field Doug said with a chuckle in his voice "What do you think would happen if we put a saucer nest over there? People would think a flying saucer had landed!"

And so it began.

Doug and Dave's relationship was very much like that of the bickering friends in

Doug Bower

Doug and Dave *in deep cover.*

Gene Saks' 1968 film *The Odd Couple*. With Doug as the fastidious, neurotic Felix Ungar and Dave the laid-back, slovenly Oscar Madison. As will become apparent from the interview, Dave loved winding Doug up.

A life-long smoker, Dave died of cancer in 1996. But Doug is still very much alive and well and, at 82, he is as fit and lucid as he ever was. Although during the interview I promised never to call him Granddad, that is exactly how I feel about him. I'm very proud to have Doug Bower as my cereological Grandfather.

THE FIELD GUIDE

The following interview took place at Doug's Southampton home in December 2005.

BEGINNINGS

What first inspired you to start creating crop circles?

On 21 October 1958, Trafalgar Day, my wife Ilene and I sailed from Tilbury on the ten pounds assisted passage to Australia. I was working nearly a hundred hours a week for thirteen pounds – that was the wages then - so I said let's go over there and see if we can better ourselves.

We stayed there for eight and a half years, brought a plot of land and built a bungalow, and it was during that time, in about 1966, that there was an article in *The Age*, a daily newspaper, about three circular marks that were found at Tully in Queensland. This interested me, I've always been that way inclined about Outer Space, UFOs and all the rest of it. According to the article, some experts from Melbourne were sent to investigate. They came back saying they were definitely UFO nests – saucer nests they called them; that is, circular impressions made by a landing UFO. And that was the last we ever heard of it.

What do you think actually happened there?

Doug Bower

Well I don't know. I find that this is typical of newspapers, you read an interesting story one minute but they never seem to follow it up, er, well except with the crop circles [laughs]. But nothing more was heard of it. There were no photographs at all, just a short explanation to say that the so called experts – and there was plenty of them in those days, just like there are now – said that it was definitely where UFOs had landed.

There was no such a thing as hoaxing or anything like that in those days. So I just took it that the report was correct, and that UFOs had landed. Well it had to be something, didn't it!

In 1968 we decided to come back to England. We settled in Southampton and found that a gallery had opened up, so we introduced ourselves to the owner. I've been painting since I was a small child and worked as a picture framer in Australia, so when the owner of this gallery asked if we'd like to take it over, we were happy to accept. We ran the gallery for 37 years in the end, right up until June 2005.

After settling into the gallery, getting things together and beginning to enjoy life again this chappy walked in one afternoon with a picture to be framed. His name was David Chorley and he introduced himself as a painter. I said "Well, I paint and you paint, that makes two of us." So we got talking, and after a while we decided to make Friday evenings our night to go out and have a drink at the pub. We could bring along the pictures we'd been painting the previous week and have a little talk about them. And this we did,

Doug *painting in his studio.*

every Friday night from 1968 to 1978, at the Percy Hobbs pub in Winchester, 10 miles from Southampton.

Just further on from Winchester are the Hampshire downs. When the summer months came, bringing the long evenings with them, we used to have a drink and then go up onto Cheesefoot Head, walking among the corn fields and up on the bridleways,

Doug Bower

Dave, *taking in the view.*

and absorb all the lovely scenery to get a bit of inspiration for our paintings.

One night when we were strolling along there we sat down on the bank and I suddenly remembered the newspaper article about the Tully saucer nests. So I told Dave about it and said "It would be a bit of a laugh if we could find a way to make circular marks in these corn fields." He said "Yeah, that sounds like quite a good idea".

THE FIELD GUIDE

We'd never talked about UFOs or anything before that, it was just an interest I had. Ilene had bought me an encyclopaedia of UFOs at Christmas time because she knew I was interested. In fact I couldn't wait for a visit from another planet. That was what I was waiting for. I figured that I was never going to live long enough to see an alien visitation, so it was up to us to get something down and make it happen for ourselves.

So, when I got back to the shop I scratched my head and wracked my brains. What could we use? The only thing I could think of was the five foot long security bar on the back door that made the workshop safe at the gallery. Using that we could both get down on our hand and knees, lifting it up together and going around in a circle. Don't matter about the security of the shop [laughs].

We went out this first night and I explained it to Dave. "Look, if we keep the right hand side of the bar stationary and the two of us kneel down and lift it up and go around, when we come around a complete circumference we've made a circle that's 10ft wide."

I tell you what, it was damned hard work! It was pretty tough on your knees, especially with the Hampshire flints on the ground. So we started off and it was quite a good bit of fun. We were down below corn level and, out of sight of the cars as they came around the corner over Cheesefoot Head. We were invisible, it was exciting. Anyway, we went around three or four times and we were amazed at the size of the circle we'd flattened down with this bar.

I'm not sure how long it took, but I said to Dave, "Look what we've done! This is sure to be spotted – it won't be long before it's on the news."

Turn the clock forward two years and still nobody had spotted them! After plenty of moaning and groaning Dave said "I've just about had a gut full of this! I'm not going to do it any longer."

"Look, keep going!" I said, "Because once they spot it we'll be well away. In the future you'll have the police controlling the traffic because there will be so much interest in it" But he said "Nobody's looking at them" [laughs].

The bar *on Doug's studio door.*

It wasn't easy getting Dave out there – he wouldn't go out if it had been raining.

THE FIELD GUIDE

He didn't want to have to walk through the wet crop and get his trousers soaked! Sometimes I had to walk up the tram-lines with a blanket in front of me to shake all the wet off the corn so it would be dry for him. I even brought him a pair of wellington boots!

What kept you motivated through these first years?

Well just the fun and the laughing that we had in doing it you see. But all that was to increase ten-fold afterwards. Because I realised what he said, that we were only doing them in flat fields where the only person that could ever see them was the tractor driver on the combine harvester when the corn was gathered in.

So anyway, one afternoon I'm out with Ilene in the car and we were driving up around Cheesefoot Head and over to our left is the Devil's Punchbowl, a natural amphitheatre about 300 feet deep. I thought to myself that's an ideal place for a circle, though it had only ever had sheep in there. But as we came around the corner I saw that they were ploughing it for the first time in goodness knows how many years.

So I turned us around in the car park and drove all the way back to Southampton to Dave's flat. [Laughs] I knocked on his door and said "I've got some good news, they're ploughing the punchbowl".

"Oh yeah," he said, "what does that mean then?" So I explained it to him and after that we couldn't wait for the corn to grow. The first crop appeared in the Punchbowl that June and we went straight down there with our iron bar. We were both still getting fed up with it though, what with all the damage to our knees from the flints.

Can you talk a bit about the tools you developed to create crop circles after using the iron bar?

Well we just had to get up off our knees, and there was only one alternative, and that was to stand up. I wracked my brains and that's when the stomper came into being. The original was two feet wide, one foot thick and about four foot long. We attached a rope rein on it so that you could put your right foot in the middle of it and hold the rein when you're in a standing position. That meant that you still keep the right hand side of it stationary and go around in a circle with it. It worked very well – there was no more damage to our legs or knees after that!

DISCOVERY

What did you call what you were doing then?

I can't remember. I don't think we had a name for it really. I know when I used to ring him up I'd say "Are we going out ringing tonight"? Not circling or anything, it was ringing. So the first time that we did one in the Punchbowl, Pat Delgado spotted it one

Doug's photo *of the Devils Punchbowl circle.*

morning going into Winchester and it was on the TV news that same evening.

Dave rang me up to tell me he'd seen it, and that was the start of it all.

Then came the first problem. We were still doing them on Friday nights, until someone pointed out that the circles seemed to be appearing every Saturday morning. The only answer was to go further afield, which we did, the longest journey being about 100 miles to Eastbourne.

Doug Bower

You see I couldn't really get out any night other than Fridays – what explanation was I going to give Ilene when I told her I was going out, if it was a Monday, Tuesday, Wednesday or Thursday? Friday nights was our night you see, so no notice was taken as far as Ilene was concerned, she always knew that we went out to the pub.

Our work was starting to appear in the newspapers by now: there were photographs, and of course the experts were beginning to emerge, which they do everywhere, don't they? But the most amusing thing was that every Sunday I used to take Ilene and her parents out for a picnic. My excuse to go and see on the Sunday what we'd done on the Friday was to tell Ilene, "I've just read a report in the paper that there's a circle been spotted down at Alfreston, near Eastbourne, we'll go down if you like and see if we can spot it". So off we'd go, of course I knew exactly where it was, I drove all through Alfreston and up the hill and I said "There it is look!". There was a car park at the top, I drew in, bought them all an ice cream and went to photograph it, because I always carried my camera with me.

Ilene didn't know what I was up to for seven years. One year as we went up the hill to the car park, the traffic was bumper to bumper all the way up the hill. People were stopping to look at our circle. "This is great", I thought. When we got to the car park, the chap who served me an ice cream said "My god, all this traffic down here, you should have been here a few days ago, they had the police here directing it. Did you see the *Daily Mail* the other day then?"

THE FIELD GUIDE

Unknown to us, when we'd crept down over the field to do this circle we were right next door to Denis Healey's (a former Chancellor of the Exchequer) house. There's a picture of Denis Healey with his camera around his neck – apparently he'd sold his photograph of our circle to the *Daily Mail* and they'd called it Healey's Comet!

We couldn't wait to see the Six O'clock news every evening. Pat Delgado and Colin Andrews were in the limelight by then. The press approached them because they seemed to have all the answers. We had to keep quiet, though of course we were laughing our heads off. I love winding people up, that's one of my pet things. The more we could stir it up, the more we wanted to get on and do some more.

Weren't you desperate to tell someone what you were doing?

Yeah, but I said to Dave when we first started this I said "No one in the world can know what we're doing, not even our wives," and he agreed.

In fact Dave's wife didn't know anything about it until she was walking up the high street in Southampton one morning when the *Today* newspaper was published, and a woman came up to her and said "Here, your husband's on the front of the newspaper!"

So as this went on I wondered how we were going to get out more nights than just Fridays. I don't know what Ilene would have said if I'd told her, "I'm going out Mondays, Tuesdays, Wednesdays..." because that's what we wanted to do you see, the more the merrier.

In the business, Ilene always kept the books, she's been a book-keeper all her life, and I used to tell her every time the car needed servicing. One time when I approached her about it she said "But the darn thing was only serviced a few weeks ago, where's all the miles coming from?" I had no alternative than to go over to my studio, which was at the rear of the premises, get all the newspaper cuttings that I'd gathered up, every report I could find about the crop circles. I had four big albums full of cuttings, photographs and things. I banged them down onto the workshop bench and said "There you are, that's where we've been going Friday nights".

She looked at them and she started turning the first album out. "This is only newspaper cuttings," she said, "I know you've been interested in all this what you've seen in the papers, but this don't tell me anything, does it?" As she turned more and more pages over, I realised I had to come clean.

"Well, that's our answer to the crop circles, it's Dave and I that's been doing it".

So I started explaining everything to her, but she wasn't having it. "I'm still not convinced. You're going to have to tell me what you're going to do and then take me out with you one night" I had no choice but to agree. We went up onto Cheesefoot Head and I said "I'll go down the field there and do this circle and then you can come back and have a look at it the next day."

Of course in the end Ilene was even designing one or two of them herself.

Doug Bower

Did you ever go out by yourself other than that time?

Yeah, I fell out with Dave during a period. Every Christmas Eve at the shop I invited Dave around for Christmas cake, mince pies and some beer, a little bit of a get together. And this one Christmas Eve he must have got drunk because he didn't turn up. I was livid and threw all the mince pies and everything into the dustbin. He said he was with his family, but I said "You always come up to me for Christmas Eve. Well if that's the case then, blow it, don't bother anymore".

So anyway the trouble was the circle season was approaching you see, and I thought to myself "Bugger it, I'll go out on my own". I did too, I did seven circles one night, from Southampton to Warminster. Yeah, crawling through the barbed wire, I was really spiteful about everything. I'm there stomping away and looking around for the headlights and everything, there's nobody to talk to. It was no fun at all. It just wasn't the same without Dave.

Eventually I went around to his flat and as he opened the door he put his hand out "Hello" he says, "How are you?" I think he was missing it as well. So we went out that very same night.

You must have been getting a bit nervous though. The more publicity the circles got, the more people were going to be out there looking for you.

THE FIELD GUIDE

Yeah, it even got to the point where people were using their summer holidays to come down from all over England to hang around Cheesefoot Head with car batteries and search lights.

Then I think the *Sunday Mirror* offered £10,000 reward for anybody who could provide the answer to the circles mystery. It was all getting a getting a bit dodgy, so we finished with Cheesefoot Head for a while and moved things into Wiltshire; Warminster and Cley Hill, which had been known as UFO hot spots since the 1960s.

Unknown to us, all the circles we made around Warminster were reported in the local papers down there, which of course we never saw. It was only later, when the likes of Terence Meaden came on the scene saying that newspapers in Warminster had reported circles there years ago.

Did you ever go up on Cradle Hill and look for UFOs yourself?

Oh yeah. Dave and I went up there. Up top there's a big farmers barn, covered with autographs and things from people who had been up there UFO watching. So we got some chalk and we drew one on there as well. A UFO with two blokes sat in it. I think that was in the late '70s, but I've lost track of time these days.

Although we did those ones around Warminster, our pet place was up near

Winchester. So we were pleased when Colin Andrews and Pat Delgado set up Operation Blackbird at Westbury. We thought about putting one down there, but someone else beat us to it, as you know. The Wizard from Bristol or Mystic Merlin, wasn't it? .

WATCHING THE WATCHERS

The time that Colin had Operation White Crow running on top of Cheesefoot Head was when I'd fallen out with Dave and was working alone. The farmer gave them permission to put the van in one of his fields, so that their cameras were pointing down into the Punchbowl.

Ilene and I always used to go out for a meal on Saturday evenings, and I really wanted to put something down for the cameras. So on our way back from the Percy Hobbs, where we would eat, we pulled into the car park at Cheesefoot Head. I could see their van down there, which was on 24 hour watch, with cameras running. So I just put a circle down in the opposite direction, right behind the cameras.

I made this lovely circle all by myself, even put a ring around it. To keep the corn standing between the main circle and the outer ring I used to hold the stomper horizontally across the corn and walk around that way, to make a mark.

Of course that got us the best publicity of all. When Colin Andrews and company came down from the van the next morning and found the circle, they said that something of higher intelligence knew that they were there. Nice of them to say that about me!

Why did you decide to put a ring around that one? Was it something you had been doing on the other circles as well?

Oh yeah, we'd even put the four satellites around some as well. We decided to make things more complicated once Terence Meaden came into the picture. If he hadn't appeared, talking about vortices and things, we would just have continued doing simple circles all the time. That's what we really wanted to do – because a UFO is supposed to be circular.

229

But with Meaden being another expert, hogging the limelight with his explanations, the vortices and so on, we decided to challenge him. So we went into the Punchbowl and made another circle a bit further out from the main circle. When the press asked Meaden about this one, he said that the vortex was hitting the side of the hill, moving back into the field and making another.

We had to do something about this. So that's why we started making the outer passages, and the passages with another circle on the end. We had no alternative, what else could we do? It was just to keep him quiet, which it did. Eventually Terence retired from the scene completely. That pleased us quite a lot. Poor old Terence, he's a nice chap but, there it was – we had to get rid of him.

Much later on we had an interview with him in a pub in Salisbury. He was very concerned when we went public. In the back of his mind he wanted proof, but he also thought that, somewhere amongst all those circles, there must be some that were genuine, that would tie in with his theories.

In fact it is possible – I've seen whirlwinds pick up whole bales of hay. The biggest one was up on Pepperbox Hill one afternoon. Ilene had just sat down with her mother to have a picnic. I went up for a stroll to the top of the hill and saw that the combine harvesters had left all their lines of straw in the fields. Suddenly I noticed a whirlwind, and it was coming right towards me. It was really frightening, like a tornado. It was picking up at least three lines left by the combine, and you know how wide apart those lines are. I've never seen anything like it, and it must have taken the straw up about 700-800ft up in the air until it finally lost power and all the straw started falling down like snow.

But of course even something like that wouldn't give your circle nice smooth edges like we did!

COMPLEXITY

How straightforward was the jump from simple circles to more

complex geometries?

Well the big puzzle first of all was how on earth did we make a straight line in the dark in a corn field? I had the bright idea of the baseball cap. I got a bit of picture framing wire hanging down from the baseball cap with a round ring on the end of it and I thought to myself if I look through that ring onto a silhouette of a tree or something on the horizon and keep my eye trained on that and walk towards it, I'm bound to keep a straight line. And it worked.

We tried it and did wonky lines with it.

Did you?!

We weren't very good at it!

Doug and Dave *using the baseball cap.*

Doug Bower

Dave had to walk behind me with his stomper. I had to walk sideways to make a mark in the corn, because the width of your shoe that way is wider than it is if you walk forward. If he kept my mark in the middle of his stomper all the way, then we could carry on and make a passageway that was as long as we wanted it to be. Then as far as the circle was concerned it was just a piece of string with one of us holding the end of it and the other marking out the perimeter. We started using that technique when we first started doing the satellite circles. The main circle and then smaller ones to the north, south, east and west. They were called the quintuplets.

What we wanted to do first of all was the legs of the spaceship. When we saw the so called experts down there with theodolites and all the rest of it, what the Ordinance Survey was using, and they were saying "It's dead accurate you know!" [laughing] It just egged us on to go and do more and more and more.

COMPETITION

We were always wondering, "what can we think up next?" But if it hadn't been for Terence Meaden, I think right from the beginning to the end it would have been just plain simple circles. Until the time that somebody up in Wiltshire did that big formation.

The one in East Field, that was used on the cover of the Led Zeppelin compilation album? Did you ever have any contact from that group, let's call

them the "A Team"?

No, didn't know them from that day to this. The thing that upset us was the night we went to Wesbury and there were one or two reporters up there. They'd come down from Gloucestershire I think. They started talking to us, asking questions, and then as we were walking up towards the top of the hill we looked down and our hearts sunk. Right next to the one that we'd done previously someone else had done one. "Aahhhhh!" I though to myself. That was the one that the *Daily Mirror* paid somebody to do one next to ours, though we didn't know that until afterwards. It was the first time we saw one that wasn't ours.

Dave said, "That's the end, I don't want to do it no more!"

But I said "No, we don't take any notice of that. Let's get back up around Winchester and carry on doing them." I was hoping against hope that he'd say yes.

I was more keen than he was you see. I took the meal out, the cheese rolls and the coffee, bought him wellington boots and waterproofs. When things started getting a bit dodgy and everybody was flocking around from all over the country keeping a vigil up there – because there was rewards being offered now you see – I thought the only solution to this was to go out on a pouring wet night.

Doug Bower

Dave said "What?!"

I said, "Look I'll get two good umbrellas and we'll go down into the punchbowl with them up". But he wasn't having any of it! It never happened!

Just to show you how keen I was, I tried to think of things we could do in the Winter. My idea was that they plant the corn at the end of the harvest season and it comes up so many inches high throughout the winter and stays that way until the warmer weather comes. So I thought that if we both had a hoe we could go into the fields in the winter months, slice off all this corn that was growing, and when the corn started to grow in the spring you'd get a complete circle with no corn at all.

I got Dave a hoe because I already had this long dutch hoe that I borrowed off Ilene's dad, who was a keen gardener. I told him that I would take the handle off and give it a good sanding! Off we went up to Cheesefoot Head with these two hoes, lovely mild night it was, and the corn was only up about three inches. We got the string and made a mark all the way around the diameter of the circle we wanted to do, then we started slicing off all the crop. But, unbeknownst to us, we were shaving it off, but the roots were still staying in the ground. As the warmer weather came, the crop grew up as if nothing had ever happened. Waste of time!

The other thing I thought of was also a non-starter. Up at Hurstbourne Tarrant in Hampshire, where I used to take Ilene and her mother for a picnic, there was some Russian hogweed (wild rhubarb) growing in a chap's garden, and in a field next door. This stuff grows to about eight feet tall, and if you touch it when it's growing you come out in blisters. At the end of the summer all their seeds drop down and thousands and thousands of more plants spring up.

Right alongside the road there was some of this growing, and it had gone to seed. So I said to Dave one night, look we'll take some plastic bags, pull up in the car, put the plastic bags over the top of the seed heads, hold them tight at the bottom, shake them like mad and we'll get a bag full of seed.

235

So that was the next operation, down into the Punchbowl in the middle of the Winter. So we went down there with the string and we made a circle, because the fields had all been sown beautifully, all rolled, lovely, flat like a billiard table. As I went round making the circle, Dave was to start scattering the seeds so we'd have a circle of eight-foot rhubarb.

But what we didn't realise was that when the farmer starts spraying in the spring-time he uses weed killer. So that was the end of that idea!

Doug Bower

INSPIRATIONS

Going back to the designs, wasn't the idea for the sidebars inspired by a surrealist painting?

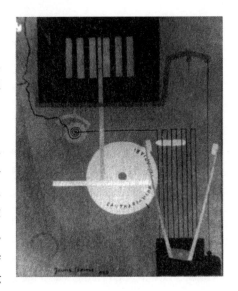

Yeah it was called Young Woman, by a Frenchman called George Ribemont-Dessaignes, from 1915 (*pictured right*). Looked nothing like a woman of course! But that gave us the idea of the four bars, two each side, I think also we also got the idea of the laddergram from a painting as well. Dave had quite a few books on modern art and nineteenth century art.

What amazed me most of all about our designs was how they coincided with the markings on rocks and things that were all done thousands of years ago. Especially by the Hopi Indians. That was the thing that puzzled me most – where was the connection? Most of these similarities only came to light when we saw them written about and pictured in books and magazines about the circles, like *The Cerealogist*.

THE FIELD GUIDE

DAVE

Well we used sit in the pub there and doodle a bit on the pack of a piece of paper, but Dave was more concerned with his pint of beer than anything else, you know. And I had to do my upmost to egg him on to keep going, for a bit of company really. He enjoyed it, because Dave lived from day to day, he had practically nothing, you see, I was always a bit better off than him.

I felt sorry for him in a way. Our Friday nights, and our other nights, it was always I'd buy him a packet of fags and a meal and wellington boots and waterproof gear to out in the fields at night because we both had a good laugh.

OK, just to show you what old Dave was like and how much of a perfectionist I am, when I used to draw out the designs of what were going to do that night, I would estimate that the main circle would be, we'll say for arguments sake, ten times around, and that would give us a diameter of such and such. That's how much I used to be into it. So old Dave used to say "Yeah, yeah". But most of the time we were down there he would never keep count of how many times he'd been around. He was half cut (drunk) half the time [laughing].

So I journeyed all the way to Weymouth one day to Chesil Beach in Dorset, you know, where all the pebbles are washed up. I thought to myself, if I gather up some nice

238

Every year *Dave used to send Doug a painting at Christmas incorporating their previous season's exploits. In the paintings they were cast not as Doug and Dave, but Bill and Ben.*

pebbles, Dave can be like a cricket umpire. To count the six overs in a match, they have six pebbles in their pocket, and at each over they pass one into the other pocket. Otherwise they'll lose count, like Dave did.

So I bring back these lovely pebbles, going backwards and forwards in the surf for hundreds of years, and I gave old Dave this collection and said "There you are, now if we're going to go around 10 times there's your five pebbles, and I'm going to be doing five as well". So he put them in his pocket and off we went. Half way through the formation I thought to myself, I'll go over and see how he's getting on. I said "How many times have you been around?" He says, "I don't know." I said "Well where's the pebbles I gave you?" He said, "I threw them away!" [laughing] He used to do it just to annoy me, to wind me up.

239

It wasn't deep seated for Dave like it was with me, you know. And of course the real reason why we eventually went public in 1991 was because Dave's health was failing, and that was about the end of it. I could see that it was no good carrying on. He didn't really live long afterwards. He died in 1996.

GOING PUBLIC

What do you think would have happened if you hadn't gone public?

Doug Bower

I would have carried on... I think. Well you know the real story as well as I do, but I'm not going to bring that up as there could be repercussions. I could have continued with it. All the time the interest was there, and the publicity was there. I suppose really when it all boils down, I was just a publicity seeker, really.

It got that way in the end, although it didn't start that way. I wanted people to believe that a UFO had landed during the night. But it's not about what we made of it, it's what other people have made of it, isn't it, the so-called experts that build themselves up in front of the cameras and the media. They're the ones with egg on their face, they're the ones who can't admit to any of the mistakes that they've made, and they never will. Even if we could prove beyond doubt that it was us that did it, there's still a group of people who will say "No, he's a liar". I've been a liar ever since 1991!

Every year since then I've been contacted by the media asking if I'd do a demonstration for them and appear on film. The Japanese wanted me to do it in vegetables. I said "There's nothing over here but swedes and turnips until the corn is up".

How did you feel when other people like myself and the other groups in Wiltshire were starting to make circles?

Well, we knew it was all over for us, because the designs that you were creating were nothing like anything we could ever achieve ourselves. Once you lot started, the mystery had gone out of it completely. I took a back seat because I knew I couldn't compete with what you were doing, I had no knowledge of how you were doing it, but I admired you for all what you were doing and I used to cut all the pictures out from the papers.

I thought to myself, "Well, we had a good time for all those 14 years, and we got a good laugh out of it, but now these chaps have taken over." I used to look at the new formations in amazement and say "My god, look what it's all come to", and wonder how you did it. Did you use lasers?

Although ours had the mystery behind it all, you created another mystery with the designs that you were doing because people were turning around to say "No human beings could ever accomplish anything like this during the dark hours".

But it pleased me, I knew very well that it was no good us carrying on because Dave was on his last legs. I was born in 1924, so I was 54 when all this it started. I could have carried on for years. I could go out now in a field and do one.

We did pole vaulting and all back in our day. Went up into Ursborne Turrant into the hazelwood to find the nice straight sticks. I cut one for Dave as well. He was putting on so much bloody weight though that he couldn't go over the crop! We used the sticks for grapeshot (smaller circles).

The best one we did was near Broughton up near Stockbridge. Nice field that was, I even drove the car into that field. Up near the radio dish at Chilbolton. You should have seen us running down the tram lines and then sticking it in and sailing over the top of the crops, it was absolutely marvellous. As you ran up the tramline, stick the stick in, jump into the standing corn, do the small grapeshot – which was about one time around with a four foot stomper, giving you an eight foot circle. And then you could take a bit of a leap from that small circle in again and go over into the crop to make the next circle, you could do the big one then. That was funny that was. But Dave had had enough of all that, he was putting on weight and he wasn't going over the stick at all like you should do, that annoyed me, he was going around the stick!

With the benefit of hindsight, is there anything you would have changed about the circles and about how it all panned out?

I think I could have done with a good PR agent. We were taken for a ride, there's no doubt about that. We were very green. We didn't get a penny for any of it. Not even from the *Sunday Mirror,* who had offered so many thousand pounds for proof. The money that we must have made for Kodak alone!

Was there ever a point when you thought it had gotten out of control,

when it exploded in the media?

The only time I got a bit worried was when Colin Andrews was going to ask the government for more funding to carry on the research. The other thing that worried me most of all, when you turn the clock back, was the fact that with all the thousands of miles that people were doing in their cars looking at the circles, all the aircraft flying over them in the evenings taking photographs, was that there might be an accident. If there had been a collision somewhere and somebody got killed, then I would have felt very very guilty about that. But it's marvellous to think that in all those years there it never happened.

And the tourist industry. Did you ever feel guilty about flattening the farmers' crop?

Dave used to feel it more than me. We used to do a big circle and old Dave used to say "My god, look at the damage we've done!" I just said, "No, let's go around another couple or three times!"

But his feelings were absolved really because a farmer told him not to worry about it, as very rarely did they lose the crop. He said they can lower the cutting blade on the combine, get right underneath it and harvest it anyway. It's just like wind damage really isn't it, and most fields get wind damage.

Doug Bower

A chap told me up there on Cheesefoot Head one day, he said 80 per cent of all the wheat that's cut in this country goes to cattle feed because it's such poor quality. He said that the breadmaking wheat comes from Canada.

In retrospect would you consider what you were doing as art? I do. I think it is art and you are my artistic hero. I think you and Dave really were the greatest artists of the twentieth century.

No! Well I consider myself quite a good artist as far as painting is concerned. Dave was an artist as well. That made two of us out in the countryside at night. But when I look at the designs for the crop circles... No it was 100 per cent fooling the public to make them believe that a flying saucer had landed. When we started making the passageways which did away with the circular part, when it started getting into that, it was taking on...

Yeah, I see what you mean! When we started doing the passageways our brains were thinking up more complex sorts of things to add to them, and I suppose really when the picture Young Woman came into it... but no, I can't say that art as I know it came into it all that much.

The best feelings of all that we got was out in the middle of a corn field at two o'clock in the morning, underneath the stars. The feeling that we got in the fields at night, right away from everybody. Everybody was in bed, we were the only two people out.

The most beautiful feeling of all that I got ever out of doing it, as I said to Dave time and time again in those first 14 years, was "Do you realise that we are the only two people on this planet that's doing this, and nobody in the world knows what's causing it? It's a wonderful feeling to be out here."

Doug and Dave *painting in the studio.*

CIRCLEMAKERS

As Summer settles over England's green and pleasant land, so her fields become a living gallery for the display of dozens of beautiful and enigmatic crop patterns. Mark Pilkington *speaks to some of the artists formerly known as UFOs, plasma vortices, rutting hedgehogs etc.*

What inspired you to first start circle making?

Rod Dickinson (RD): The gradual realisation that the formations were the work of human hands (in 1991) inevitably led to my first attempt at making a circle. I remember being convinced we had made a horrible mess, and I began to think I had been wrong, and that people could not in fact be responsible for any of the patterns, until I saw the

A shortened version of this interview appeared in Fortean Times magazine, July 2000.

local paper a couple of days later... A well-known local investigator claimed our horrible mess had all the hallmarks of the "genuine" phenomenon; bent-but-not-broken-stalks, flowing crop-lay etc.

My view of the circles, the people or groups that attend them, and the media was turned upside down. Almost immediately after I had made this circle I realised that there was an extraordinary space that could be - and was best - occupied by artists. Later that year of course I realised that I was following in the foot steps of Doug and Dave, and other circlemaking groups.

John Lundberg (JL): Curiosity and the chance to extend my art practice outside the gallery walls. Initially I was quite willing to believe that many of the circles were of non-human origin, and I was initially sceptical of Doug and Dave's 1991 confession in *Today* newspaper. But events such as the 1992 Crop Circle Making Competition initiated by Rupert Sheldrake, and Jim Schnabel's book *Round in Circles,* helped convince me that it was indeed possible to create complex man-made patterns overnight.

The main catalyst for me was meeting Rod. We decided to formalise a group committing the necessary time, money and energy that allowed us to see just how far we could push the envelope in terms of the scale and complexity of the formations we created. The possibility of creating an artefact that may well be interpreted as being of non-human origin was an intriguing proposition.

THE FIELD GUIDE

Wil Russell (WR): For me it was visiting a circle that appeared in my home village. It captured my imagination with regard to the UFO phenomena – the fact I could be so near to a landing site for a craft really resonated with me. Then, having seen the media exposé of Doug & Dave, I wondered if I could possibly make something closely resembling one of these landing sites.

Rob Irving (RI): Initially, I made circles to test the claims made by so-called "experts" that we, mere earthlings, are incapable of creating anything so large and complex given the time and conditions in which they appear. The only way to surely know was to try it myself. After that I was inspired by pure artistic impulse; it can be a very powerful experience.

Do you think that the sense of mystery around crop circles has faded in the last few years? If so, what's the role of the circlemaker in the current climate?

RD: Perhaps in the eyes of the media circles are perceived differently to

Circlemakers

the way that they were ten years ago. But there is still a large core group of people who invest enormously in the circles - with their own journals, conferences and lecture tours. It is their beliefs that fascinate me.

JL: I think there is always going to be a residual belief in the non-human origins of crop circles. The media's interest in circles undoubtedly took a nose dive after Doug and Dave's revelations, but since then I think the sheer scale and complexity of many of the formations causes many people to question once again if they could indeed be of non-human origin. In recent years we have seen patterns of mind-boggling complexity appearing, spanning 1000 ft and incorporating hundreds of individual circles.

I've met several people who have no real interest in the circles and who are quite happy to believe that I may have created some of them over the years. But suggesting to these same people that every crop circle formation is man-made usually elicits disbelief.

Although it may seem contradictory to our perceived agenda, undoubtedly one of our roles is to encourage belief in the non-human origin of the circles. Doug & Dave's claim to original authorship and our subsequent claims have created an atmosphere well known to theological sociologists – that disconfirmation can lead to strengthened belief. For those who want to believe, there are enough soft edges on our activities to allow their beliefs to perpetuate. We never lay claim to specific formations; we only claim authorship of formations in the round.

THE FIELD GUIDE

To some croppies our claims to authorship are as akin to those made by hoax callers who claim responsibility for actions they haven't committed, like people claiming to be the Yorkshire Ripper. The more paranoid believer can weave intricate conspiracy theories around us, casting us as shady disinformation agents in the pay of the government, fighting against the rising tide of New Age belief... or some such narrative.

WR:　　Our role is to continue to push the boundaries of what people think is humanly possible.

RI:　　People's beliefs might fluctuate, but often the most irrational are the most resilient to change.

What do you think drives those who still seek mystery in your art?

RD:　　The circles function as what Alfred Hitchcock called a MacGuffin – the thing that propels the plot along, evoking a whole set of desires and beliefs and the promise of something bigger. In this way the circles confuse the distinction between reality and representation. They create rumours, tantalising narratives, something you can't be sure about.

JL:　　The circles have become signs and portents of our time, huge Rorschach tests writ large on the fields of England. The circle-prone area of Wiltshire is peppered with sacred sites. The circles themselves can be viewed as temporary sacred sites where people gather to meditate on their meaning, imbuing them with mystical and mythic significance. These people are helping to extend the meaning and reach of the formations which, in this context, can be viewed as mass participation artworks.

WR: That something fantastic is happening which they can be part of.

RI: The mystery of their own existence - the art mirrors our dreams.

People claim to have experienced a wide variety of anomalous phenomena while inside one of your formations. How does this make you feel and what does it say to you about the nature of such phenomena?

RD: I have a materialist view of the immaterial and the paranormal, not through scepticism or disbelief but because as an artist I deal in "things" and the representation of things. One might expect the circles, as a MacGuffin, to generate all kinds of impossible situations – so I do not find it surprising that people should want to reinforce their beliefs with this type of anomalous experience.

Sometimes people have an intense response to the circle they are visiting – a response to an artwork in effect – but not recognising it as an artwork they interpret their experience more literally as a paranormal experience.

THE FIELD GUIDE

JL: I do not have an explanation, other than that consciously – ie. hoaxing footage, inventing stories – or unconsciously, these people want to contribute and participate in the evolution of our artworks and the associated mythology.

WR: I feel happy that I've been able to contribute to someone's well being, on whatever level that might transpire. I do not feel there is anything strange going on if people feel particular sensations or "paranormal" experiences from a piece of my work. In fact, we are no strangers to transcendental experiences ourselves, we just witness them from a different perspective.

RI: It reminds me of the extent to which "anomalous" experience is generated within. I am more entertained by those who try to force such phenomena into a scientific framework – the need to "know" and explain to others, which tells me a lot about ego.

Would you place circle making within any particular artistic tradition?

JL: I see our work as the continuation of an unseen tradition of artists working covertly in the realm of the paranormal, from the Turin Shroud to the Roswell "Alien Autopsy" film. Back in 1988 the Turin Shroud was carbon-dated proving that it was not the ancient relic many had hoped it to be, but instead an artefact of the 11th or 12th century.

Circlemakers

In their book *The Turin Shroud: In Whose Image?*, Lynn Picknet and Clive Prince argue that the anonymous author of the shroud may well have been Leonardo da Vinci. He was known to have no love for those who worshipped relics: "Many are those who trade in tricks and simulated miracles, duping the foolish multitude; and if nobody unmasked their subterfuge, they would impose them on everyone." I see our work following in the footsteps of the creators of the Shroud – whoever they were.

In tandem to this I also see our work in the tradition of "Ostensive Performance". Ostention is a term borrowed from semiotics, referring to the communication of information through actions rather than words. Folklorist Bill Ellis uses it to describe the point at which legend becomes real and reality becomes legend. He describes how on numerous occasions individuals or groups have perpetrated Ostensive Performances of certain legends, causing them to cross over from folklore into perceived reality.

THE FIELD GUIDE

RI: On one level – especially in the UK, and Wiltshire in particular – it is a concentration of large-scale land art; a decoration of the landscape using natural and available materials – not far removed from what... say, Andy Goldsworthy or Richard Long, or even our prehistoric ancestors might create. That is from the artist's perspective, but then the viewer's reaction takes the work into the realm of devotional art. Again, this connects with equally long and similarly creative traditions. The formations inspire the same sense of sanctity, awe and magic we feel when we experience a cathedral or other sacred site.

To elaborate on the idea of mimicking the divine... Crop circles act as a magnet to the type of people who equate their own sense of wonder with divinity.

Circlemakers

To these otherwise intelligent people – for various reasons, I suspect they include a high proportion of academics and scientists – the role of the human hand, the artist, is considered sinister and illicit. The more a person trusts his own judgement in such matters the less he is inclined to accept that his perception has been affected through magic. Visionaries tend to turn away from the mundanity of earthly explanation in favour of an interest in themselves, of their own subjectivity. Thus, if one is awe-struck by the otherworldliness of something then it must be, literally, otherworldly.

This mix of creative subjectivity and the claustrophobically objective has its downside, though. When circlemakers famously attempted to persuade an audience of croppies that humans are perfectly capable of manufacturing wonder by producing wonderful things – the ceiling of St Peter's in Rome, for example – they confused the collective certainty of *knowing* that as far as crop circles are concerned, this cannot be true: "You are not artists, you are scum!" was the reply.

Similar disparity must have fashioned the medieval notion of the artist sleeping while the angels did his work, thereby excusing the viewer's own sense of wonderment in the face of obvious practicality. Likewise, it has been mooted – not very loudly – that circlemakers are capable of creating such masterpieces only whilst under the direct influence of some higher power. In rejecting the human artist, this purely devotional response to art becomes an antidote to our preoccupation with authorship; the artwork is much more powerful for being created anonymously… *magically.*

THE FIELD GUIDE

Sometimes, self-conferred arbiters of taste and judgement reject new ideas simply because they are new or unheard of. In the sphere of contemporary art, two people can do identical artworks and one might be considered a work of genius with the other seen as poor, simply because of who has made it. This condition is prevalent but makes little sense aesthetically or experientially; it has no real value other than to give us some idea of consensus.

Meanwhile, in life, perception is shaped by the local and cultural environment in much the same way as a theatrical environment shapes our perception of a performance. Outside the "correct" context, our experiences are no longer governed by familiar or given conditions. There exists a much more practical relationship between art and perception, and it is no surprise that it triggers "paranormal" experience. The same transaction can be traced through traditions of sympathetic magic and its laws of similarity and contact: Draw a circle around a stone and the stone becomes the incarnation of mystery. Similarly, if we adorn an image with belief – as ufologists are inclined to do, for instance – it ultimately defines our belief; our interpretation acts to model our vision of what god and our future "should" look like.

Russia had its first crop circle in 2000, in Yuzhnoye near Stavropol. How do you feel about this global spread? Does it bother you that the quality of some newer designs is not up to the standard of your own work?

Circlemakers

RD: The crop circle phenomenon is like a strange sociological equation, with a number of key components. Somewhere in that equation sits a viral structure that encourages the idea of circle making to be replicated by different, disparate groups. In that respect nobody controls the genre of circle making. This is clearly evident in the "evolution" of the designs of crop formations over the last decade – from simple circles to designs that reference non-linear mathematics and fractals. No one individual group is responsible for that development. Nor do any groups sit down and compare notes. Each development is expanded and improved by another circle making group once they have seen it in the field. That circles appear in Russia with exactly the same sort of media reaction that the circles received here ten years ago seems to me to be a clear demonstration of this same mechanism.

JL: I am rather envious of circlemakers in other countries. Expectations about the size and complexity of formations that appear in the UK are now very high, whereas the rather shabby looking Russian formation made the national news. Even Vasily Belchenko, deputy secretary of the Russian Security Council, was on site gushing about its origin: "There is no doubt that it was not man-made..." he was quoted as saying, "an unknown object definitely landed there." If the formation had appeared in the UK it would be virtually ignored by researchers and the media.

WR: Everyone has to learn somewhere. Maybe the novices still believe an extraterrestrial force is at work – I remember making my first circle and thinking that they must be created by mysterious forces, as it was so much hard work and trouble for humans to do it.

RI: When I'm not feeling purely ambivalent I am sometimes disappointed, but that only reflects my own artistic taste and prejudice. I have been known to underestimate important art movements in the past and this worries me; aesthetic judgement is always arbitrary and should be undermined - for all I know "messy" is brilliant.

How do you feel about people who exploit your work for their own ends, be they spiritual or material?

RD: I find other people's beliefs far more fascinating than my own, so I am always happy to see beliefs or spiritual pursuits manifest because of our work. It is part of the function of the circles as I see them. My exhibitions attempt to catalogue bits of these processes: the responses that the researchers have to these designs – engaging a whole host of participants who have no conscious interest in art and often do not even realise they are studying artworks – evoking all kinds of extraordinary theories and stories. These are the things that really constitute crop circles, and make them an interesting subject for an artist.

JL: Our work is there to be exploited. Without public interest in our formations they would go unnoticed, as did the efforts of Doug and Dave for many years. They were on the verge of giving up just before their formations hit

the headlines. The crop circle researchers and the media act as agents for our work, helping to propagate it and it's associated myths around the globe.

WR:　　This is all part and parcel of the phenomena. You provide the blueprints for someone to use for whatever creative or exploitative means they wish – it is their expression. To complain would expose your own work as fraudulent.

RI:　　It provides a valuable lesson in accepting other people's ideas. However, it gets a bit hard to take when they try and force them upon you.

THE FIELD GUIDE

Is it ever frustrating being unable to claim ownership of your work?

RD: Perhaps in many senses we don't own them. They are the result of a symbiotic process between circlemakers and researchers, a kind of supply and demand. As long as there are people prepared to invest emotionally in circles I am sure there will always be others who feel driven to make them.

JL: Some years ago the art critic John McEwen mused that the great thing about art, "is that no one can define it, even if we all know vaguely what it means." He proposed that the circles be viewed in this way.

Circlemakers

What differentiates a crop circle from a piece of land art is an act of perception. There is also the question of authorship. To equate crop circles with art is to undermine their mystery, their resonant significance of something unknown. For a circle to remain "genuine" it must by extension remain authorless. The circles were never intended to be viewed as works of art, but somewhat paradoxically they were made by artists.

Drained of their mystery the circles become mere specimens. But circlemaking is undoubtedly a creative act. So we are left with a paradox: The circles are created anonymously by artists, but to be effective they must not be viewed as art.

WR: It doesn't bother me, but when people aim so much hatred and vitriol towards you, it is sometimes difficult to keep your thoughts to yourself. Sometimes silence is the best answer.

RI: No. There is a lesson here too, about our obsession with authorship, and how we measure the value of art by its author. With paranormal artifice it is too interesting to witness the reaction to mystery to spoil it by claiming authorship. And besides, what's the big deal? We made it: so what? When you are responsible for making something this amazing you do not really need the validation that authorship is supposed to bring.

263

AFTERWORD

In preparing this text, I have drawn from earlier writings: previous versions of *The Beginner's Guide to Crop Circle Making* (much of the first draught that John Lundberg and I banged out between laughing fits on an afternoon in 1994 survives intact), and my "Strange Attractors", "Art and Artifice" and "The Mystery Business" articles for *Fortean Times* magazine. I see it as an expanding study that I hope will keep on growing.

Of course, given limited space, expansion in one area means shrinkage in another. A fuller version of this story would include such cerealogical gems as the "H-Glaze" saga, how the myth-cum-scientific fact that "genuine" crop circles contain magnetic dust originated, and a detailed account of Colin Andrews heroic brushes with Scottish agents of the powers-that-be. It would also include Mark Pilkington's discovery of a "pictogram" in the 1974 BD (Before Doug) entomological sci-fi flick *Phase IV*. And it would not be complete without checking on self-styled mystic Freddy Silva's latest musings, some of them channelled from Higher Sources, that since his move to America in 2005 the UK circles have been mostly "hoaxes", thus confirming our earlier observation that a circle's "genuineness" can often be measured by how well it fits an expert's teachings.

Alas, whilst pursuing this angle I promised Paul Vigay, Silva's creative advisor, that I would hold off critiquing his "Checksum" theory of how to tell non-man-made crop circles from their dubious counterparts until he formally publishes it, if he ever does. Suffice to say that crop circles will always reflect man's struggle for certainty over ambiguity, providing rehearsal-space for believers to act out what they nervously imagine certainty to be.

I would like to thank all those featured here for being so interesting, and in many cases pleasant about it. So where are they now?

Doug Bower and Ilene are living happily ever after. As does, we hear, Pat Delgado. Less so, apparently, Colin Andrews, who recently offered his crop circles database for sale on eBay, with a reserve of $250,000 – there were no takers. News of this saw him threatening to sue a regional UK newspaper for describing him as "broke". Perhaps a little bent, we say, but not broke! But such is the lot of visionaries, that their shamanic descent can continue much deeper than anticipated. We wish Colin and his wife Synthia well.

Having worked his way up the editorial hierarchy of *Flying Saucer Review* George Wingfield went off our radar completely, as, since the demise of the CCCS, has Michael Green. Thankfully, though, not Lucy Pringle, who continues to regale *Daily Mail* readers with her scientific breakthroughs, backed by a nice line in aerial views of the circlemakers' work, which she photographs herself. Likewise, John Michell, through his books and lectures has continued his studies into its mathematical, geometric and gematriac value.

Even today, with the patterns far removed from the simple circles that so captured his imagination in 1980, Dr Terence Meaden still makes occasional public pleas for the circle makers to stop, or at least agree a moratorium so that he may study the genuine phenomenon described in *JMet* without having his head turned. Talking of *JMet* contributors, who knows where my old friend Rita Goold is, and in what shape or form? She is a rare spirit and I miss her stories.

Sadly, Montague Keen fell silent in a way that seemed most fitting to him, whilst asking a question during a public debate on telepathy. He so wanted things to be true, and I hope for him they are.

As I write, just as Lt Commander Bruce's impatience towards crop circles was effective in pushing them north to Alton Barnes in 1990, the phenomenon appears to be spreading away from Ground Zero into other parts of Wiltshire and beyond, encouraged by local farmers who have collectively agreed to mow any circles on sight. Perhaps one day it will revert to occasional, relatively small outbreaks in the vicinity of Warminster and the Wiltshire/Hampshire border, echoing a time, not so long ago, when an unassuming man saw magic in communion with our mystical landscapes and acted upon it.

Rob Irving
Somerset, England 2006

THE FIELD GUIDE

INDEX

THE FIELD GUIDE

PHOTO CREDITS

Strange Attractor Press 2006
www.strangeattractor.co.uk
BM SAP, LONDON, WC1N 3XX